FIRED UP *or* [...]

"An enthralling and impressive work. I am completely convinced that the basic precepts in this book will stand the test of time for many centuries to come, indeed, probably forever. It shows how to empower people and create great societies, corporations, and cultures. I'm giving it to everyone at my own firm."

—Russell Reynolds Jr., Founder and Former CEO,
Russell Reynolds Associates, and Chairman, The Directorship Search Group

"In our turbulent times, leaders who are searching for ways to develop a healthy work environment that releases the energy of their people—releases the human spirit—could not find a more inspiring support than this great new resource for leaders in the corporate, government, and social sectors. *Fired Up or Burned Out* will be the indispensable leadership guide for leaders everywhere."

—Frances Hesselbein, Chairman and Founding President,
The Peter Drucker Foundation (renamed the Leader to Leader Institute)

"Reading this book is like having a great conversation; new and interesting people join in along the way, adding their own personal and varied insights and encouraging an increasingly smart and useful dialogue. Readers are compelled to emerge smarter, more thoughtful, and more energized and engaging with this book."

—Regina Fazio Maruca, Former Senior Editor,
Harvard Business Review, and Coauthor, *Your Leadership Legacy*

"A fabulous book, a must-read! People are hungry to learn more about the one-to-one connection to enhance their businesses and lives. Read Michael's book and learn from others who are successfully making the human connection a reality in their businesses."

—Jack Mitchell, Chairman and CEO of Mitchells/Richards/Marshs, and Author of *Hug Your Customers: The Proven Way to Personalize Sales and Achieve Astounding Results*

"Through fascinating stories, *Fired Up or Burned Out* convinced me of the power of connection—in life and in work. It helped me see what is missing in so many organizations. Just as important, I learned what to do about it."

—Marian Chapman Moore, Professor and Academic Director, Darden MBA for Executives, Darden Graduate School of Business, University of Virginia

"One of the things I've learned is that for employees to stage engaging experiences for a company's customers, they have to be engaged themselves in that company and what it stands for. Read *Fired Up or Burned Out*, and Michael Stallard will show you exactly how to ignite their passion by connecting them to your purpose."

—B. Joseph Pine II, Coauthor, *The Experience Economy*, and Cofounder, Strategic Horizons LLP

"This is a must-read for any leader or anyone aspiring to be in a leadership role. Lessons drawn uniquely from acclaimed personalities of the past become the foundation for strong leadership in tomorrow's world. There's no other book like it."

—Richard Murphy, Founder and Former CEO, ODI International

"The greatest assets in an organization are the employees, and engaging them is the most direct way to improve your business. *Fired Up or Burned Out* clearly outlines how executives can focus their energies, not only to improve their individual leadership abilities but also to add to the effectiveness of the entire team in achieving the organization's goals."

—E. Pendleton James, Chairman, Pendleton James Associates, and Former Assistant to President Reagan for Presidential Personnel

"There are few business leaders who understand the power of human connection. Given the shifting demographics in this country, it must be understood that virtually all people have the potential to achieve sufficiently to succeed in life. The broad principles and concepts in this book provide me with hope that American business leaders might begin to understand that all people have the potential to learn enough so that they have met the thresholds of competition in the global community. It is a renewed belief in humankind's capacity that provides the wellspring of what others can begin to follow. If our hope is for a world that provides fair opportunities for individuals, companies, and their communities, then we must be determined to work to make it so. Those companies that embrace the principles advocated in *Fired Up or Burned Out* will ultimately reap the benefits of successful competition in the new 'flat world.'"

—Eric J. Cooper, Ed.D., President, National Urban Alliance for Effective Education

"*Fired Up or Burned Out* is a must-read for anyone in a leadership role. Leadership can seem so complex and often times confusing when, in fact, following 'core principles' that focus on the 'basic needs' of every individual will always guide a leader to the truth! This book describes these core principles and basic needs in an easy-to-remember model that should be displayed on every leader's desk. The model is beautifully explained and wonderfully illustrated by examples of great leaders throughout history in every walk of life."

—Keith A. VanderVeen, Midwest Regional President,
Wachovia Securities, LLC

"Stallard's strategy gives business owners the tools to energize and strengthen their employees. *Fired Up or Burned Out* is a must-read for leaders who are looking for new ways to inspire spirit in the workplace."

—Shep & Ian Murray, Co-Founders and CEOs of Vineyard Vines
www.vinyardvines.com

FIRED UP *or* BURNED OUT

How to Reignite Your Team's Passion, Creativity, and Productivity

MICHAEL LEE STALLARD
with Carolyn Dewing-Hommes and Jason Pankau

THOMAS NELSON
Since 1798

NASHVILLE DALLAS MEXICO CITY RIO DE JANEIRO BEIJING

Published in Nashville, TN, by Thomas Nelson. Thomas Nelson is a trademark of Thomas Nelson, Inc.

Thomas Nelson, Inc. titles may be purchased in bulk for educational, business, fund-raising, or sales promotional use. For information, please e-mail SpecialMarkets@ThomasNelson.com.

Library of Congress Catalog-in-Publication Data

Stallard, Michael Lee.

Fired up or burned out : how to reignite your team's passion, creativity, and productivity / Michael Lee Stallard ; with Carolyn Dewing-Hommes and Jason Pankau.

p. cm.

Includes bibliographical references.

ISBN-13: 978-1-59555-281-5

1. Employee motivation. 2. Leadership. 3. Mentoring in business. I. Dewing-Hommes, Carolyn. II. Pankau, Jason. III. Title.
HF5549.5.M63S68 2007
658.3'14--dc22

2007001645

Printed in the United States of America
08 09 10 QW 5 4 3 2

To our wonderful families and friends.
Being with you brings us much joy and encouragement.

CONTENTS

PART III

The Fire Starts with You: Become a Person of Character and Connection to Ignite the Team Around You

PART IV

Learn from Twenty Great Leaders Over Twenty Days

CONTENTS

INTRODUCTION

What fires up people and helps them and the organizations they work in thrive? I'm not talking about motivational speeches and incentives that produce a short-term burst of enthusiasm. I mean, what really makes people perform to the best of their abilities for long periods of time? What causes individuals to put their hearts in their work?

Although people generally enter their organizations fired up, over time most work environments reduce that inner fire from a flame to a flicker. As I will explain, solving this problem needs to be one of the highest priorities of today's organizations.

In this book you will learn how to increase the fire and passion inside people that is necessary for individuals and organizations to achieve their potential. The approach I will describe is based on the results of E Pluribus Partners' multiyear study of leaders who succeeded and those who failed to engage the people they led. Our work draws upon explanations and insights identified from diverse fields of knowledge, including psychology, sociology, neuroscience, political science, organizational behavior, systems theory, history, philosophy, and religion.

One of the best ways to learn how to fire up people is to study the best practices of outstanding leaders. The leaders you'll learn from include these:

- a renowned basketball coach whose Hall of Fame biography credits him for producing teams that "scaled unprecedented heights that no future organization in any sport is likely to approach"
- a remarkable twenty-five-year-old queen in the 1500s with no leadership experience who inherited a bankrupt England and led her country to become one of the most powerful nations on earth
- an exceptional woman who began as a volunteer in her organization, then went on as CEO to transform it into one of the best-managed organizations worldwide, according to the late Peter Drucker
- a distinguished American career soldier who was awarded the Nobel Peace Prize, named *Time* magazine's Man of the Year twice, and was considered by Winston Churchill to be the primary architect of the Allies' victory during World War II

These are just a few of the remarkable people whose stories will help you understand how to fire up people in your organization.

Do You Thrive or Just Survive?

How many people truly thrive at work? Research by the Gallup Organization suggests that fewer than three in ten Americans are engaged in their jobs.[1] In other countries, the number is even lower. Just imagine the wasted human potential! Because so few individuals are thriving in organizations, it follows that organizations are wasting much of their potential too.

Over the course of my twenty-five-year business career, there have been times when I thrived and others when I merely survived. In a couple of the worst instances, the work culture slowly drained the life out of me. So there you have it: thrive, survive, or die. Which term describes what your work culture is doing to you? If you are a leader, how would the people who report to you answer that question?

I've been interested in work cultures throughout my career because I wanted to understand the culture that would bring out the best in me. My interest increased dramatically in the late 1990s when I became the chief marketing officer for the global private wealth management business of a major international brokerage firm on Wall Street. In that position, I recognized that a key success factor for our business was building strong relationships between our clients and our firm's frontline professionals, and I did whatever was possible to promote such relationship building. In addition, we developed and implemented business practices to keep our frontline professionals fired up. The result was that our revenues doubled over a two-and-a-half-year period, and our business achieved its first billion-dollar revenue year in the firm's history. During that time I realized that my colleagues and I had discovered something special.

In the spring of 2002, I left Wall Street to start a think tank to assist people and organizations in achieving their potential. In the search to comprehend every aspect of how to help people thrive in organizations, I learned from the advice and insights of experts in a broad range of fields, and from the approaches of great and failed leaders. My coauthor Carolyn Dewing-Hommes shared with me her insights gained from a Citibank study when she had access to some of the world's most prominent companies and their leaders. My other coauthor, Jason Pankau, shared insights that he developed as a leader and a coach of corporate leaders. One important insight emerged from two experiences that forever changed my life.

The Power of Connection

My wife was diagnosed with breast cancer in late 2002. Fortunately, it was detected early, removed by surgery, and treated with radiation. While Katie underwent treatments at our local hospital, the kindness and compassion of many health-care workers comforted us. Some of them were cancer survivors. They knew what we were going through, and they went beyond their regular duties to make a human connection with us. Those connections boosted our spirits.

Twelve months later, Katie was diagnosed with cancer again, this time ovarian. During the first half of 2004, Katie had six chemotherapy treatments. She took a break from chemo over the summer, then started high dosage chemotherapy at Memorial Sloan-Kettering Cancer Center in New York City. Our experience there really surprised me. Every time we approached the front doors of the Fifty-third Street entrance in midtown Manhattan, the exuberant doormen locked their eyes on us and greeted us with big, warm smiles as if we were friends coming to visit. The receptionist and security people were equally friendly. At our first office visit, Dr. Martee Hensley, Katie's oncologist, spent an hour educating us and answering a long list of questions. Although the statistics were sobering, Dr. Hensley's warm disposition and optimistic attitude lifted our spirits and gave us hope. Simply put, the connection with the people at Sloan-Kettering encouraged us.

One day while Katie was having a treatment, I went to the gift shop to get something to drink and stumbled on a meeting in the adjacent lounge where Sloan-Kettering employees were discussing an employee survey. I overheard them share that they loved working there because they loved their colleagues, their patients, and their cause, which is to provide what is stated on the center's printed materials . . . *the best cancer care, anywhere.* It was apparent that those health-care professionals had formed a connection with one another and with their patients. During our time at Memorial Sloan-Kettering, I witnessed more joy, trust, cooperation, and connection there than in 95 percent of the offices I had been in over my career. Who would have guessed that a cancer treatment center could be such a vibrant and positive work environment?

Today, I'm overjoyed to say, Katie is in remission for both cancers, and she feels great. Reflecting on those days, I'm convinced that the connection we felt from the tremendous outpouring of care provided by health-care workers, friends, and family helped Katie overcome cancer, and it protected our family's spirits. An American Cancer Society publication stated that feeling alone is one of the worst things for cancer patients. We rarely felt alone because we were constantly reminded that many, many people were pulling for us. We figured people were praying for us from probably every religion known to man, and even our atheist friends said they were sending positive thoughts our way. Perhaps for the first time in my life, I experienced the joy that comes from a real sense of community and connection to people beyond my family and close circle of friends.

For years I did not fully appreciate or understand the importance of relationships and connection. There is increasing evidence that this is a national problem. The well-documented decline in joy following World War II in the midst of growing economic prosperity is widely believed to be attributable to diminishing connection in our lives: families have spread out geographically, more families have become headed by two-career couples, and more time has been spent in the workplace. Two books by respected authorities in their fields, psychologist David Myers's *American Paradox*[2] and political scientist Robert Lane's *The Loss of Happiness in Market Democracies*,[3] describe this phenomenon. In the pages ahead, I will shed light on this problem and how we can correct it.

Connection After 9/11

Another insight about our environment's impact on us came to me as I considered what I felt on the mornings following the terrorist attacks on September 11, 2001. Walking from Grand Central Station to my office near Times Square, I vividly remember looking down the canyon-like avenues and seeing American flags flying everywhere against the backdrop of a giant smoldering cloud that hovered over the southern end of Manhattan. I also recall New Yorkers nodding and making eye contact with me as if to say, "We'll make it through this." (If you've been to New York City, you know that making eye contact with strangers is rare.)

A sense of connection in our shared belief in freedom and democracy moved the hearts of people across America to fly their flags and send money for the families who lost loved ones. And connection moved rescue workers and volunteers to come to New York City and Washington, D.C., to do what they could to help. Although New Yorkers pride themselves on individualism, I can tell you they were profoundly moved by the outpouring of affection from their fellow Americans. During that time of shock, of mourning, and of sadness, the empathy and compassion extended by people throughout the United States and the rest of the world provided the healing embrace New Yorkers needed to continue on.

Social commentator David Brooks, writing about American unity following September 11, likened us to one big family because even though we may have our differences, when one of our own is in trouble, we are there for one another.[4] The same strength of connection got us through the Depression and World War II.

The sense of connection I felt following the 9/11 terrorist attacks had a profound effect on me. It led Carolyn, Jason, and me to name our think tank E Pluribus Partners, inspired by America's motto *E Pluribus Unum,* which in Latin means "out of many, one." John Adams, Benjamin Franklin, and Thomas Jefferson chose that phrase. If they had seen Americans coming together in the aftermath of 9/11, I believe they would have stood up and cheered.

We Must Connect with Others to Thrive

The more we reflected on our own experiences and the more research we conducted about what makes people and organizations thrive, the more Carolyn, Jason, and I became convinced that it came down to this: connection. Our connection with others in our organization keeps us fired up for long periods of time. Connection meets basic human psychological needs for respect, recognition, belonging, autonomy, personal growth, and meaning. When these needs are met, we thrive. Research shows that when connection is present, organizations are more productive, more innovative, and more profitable. Our lives, including the time we spend working, are enriched with greater connection. My hope is that you will recognize the vital role of connection in reaching your personal potential and experiencing life at its best.

Conversely, the lack of connection will gradually burn us out. Organizational environments where connection is low or absent diminish our physical and mental health. They create a low level of toxicity that drains our energy, poisons our attitudes, and impacts our ability to be productive. Like the frog in the proverbial kettle of water that is oblivious to the fact that the water is slowly coming to a boil, a person in a low-connection environment had better wise up to his situation before it's too late.

In addition to bringing out the best in individual performance, connection improves group performance. Research has proven that connection makes us better problem solvers, more creative, more trusting, and more cooperative. Trust and cooperation are the lubrication, if you will, that make the tasks of organizations run better. In a work environment that fails to increase individual engagement and connection among people, results will eventually suffer. Too often that's exactly what happens when leaders experience success for a time, only to see their organization's performance decline.

Creating the right work environment requires paying attention to the so-called soft aspects of organizations. These are emotional issues such as the meaning of work and the way people treat one another. A 2004 study of fifty thousand employees at fifty-nine global companies conducted by the Corporate Leadership Council, a unit of the prestigious Corporate Executive Board, found that emotional factors were four times more effective in increasing employee engagement than rational factors.[5]

It would be rational, then, to take a hard line on the soft issues that have been overlooked in the past. While our human natures may lead us to assume that other people think the way we do (or at least they should), those who have studied personality and neuroscience tell us that people are wired very differently. The overwhelming majority of leaders with whom I have dealt excelled in left brain-directed linear and analytic thinking yet were less sensitive to the issues that had an emotional effect on people, a cognitive strength primarily directed by the right brain hemisphere.[6] (According to the research of one psychologist—based on his study of more than 2,245 executives—95 percent of them who completed the Myers-Briggs Type Indicator, a test that identifies temperament, were classified as left brain-directed "thinkers" rather than right brain-directed "feelers."[7]) Herein lies the challenge. Because of the left brain's dominance in most leaders, they tend to view actions that improve engagement and connection as inefficient and therefore unimportant, and they discount the feelings of people with other temperaments. Such leaders will be persuaded that investing in the soft issues is beneficial only when they see proof of its positive, tangible effect on the performance of people and organizations. My hope is that the following pages will persuade leaders with facts and testimonies that economic and organizational benefits come from the soft issues.

The Competitive Advantage of Connection

Building organizational connection is already happening in many revered companies. From Main Street to Wall Street, I am encouraged to see leaders beginning to recognize the value of connection and fostering a sense of community. The Ritz-Carlton Hotel Company, Starbucks, and jetBlue are very intentional about increasing their connection among employees and with customers. Harley-Davidson has created a community around its motorcycle riders, employees, and management, and the company sponsors cross-country trips and road rallies. On Wall Street, Goldman Sachs has enhanced and expanded its leadership training in order to advance the connection among its leaders. Goldman has even made leadership training available to the up-and-coming leaders of its client companies to strengthen its connection with them before the promising leaders reach the top jobs. In San Francisco, the biotech company Genentech, which *Fortune* magazine named in 2005 as the number-one-rated company to work for, brings in cancer patients to connect with its employees, throws weekly parties for employees to connect with one another, and celebrates big product breakthroughs with company-wide parties that have featured entertainers Elton John, Mary J. Blige, and Matchbox 20.[8] Southwest Airlines learned that its performance at the gate improved when it maintained a 10 to 1 frontline employee-to-supervisor ratio because supervisors could connect with, coach, and encourage those people.[9] (Some airlines have frontline employee-to-supervisor ratios of 40 to 1 that make connection difficult to maintain.)

Ed Catmull, the head of Pixar Animation Studios, formed Pixar as an antidote to the disconnection that is the norm in the film industry where independent contractors come together for a specific project and then disband upon the project's conclusion.[10] Pixar keeps the team together so that they build connection. Catmull also created the in-house Pixar University to increase connection across Pixar. At Pixar University connection occurs when every employee, from the janitors to Catmull himself, spends four hours each week in classes with colleagues learning about the arts and animation and about each other. It's no coincidence that Pixar University's crest bears the Latin phrase *Alienus Non Dieutius,* which means "alone no longer."[11]

The bottom line is that connection is a necessity to any organization that aspires to achieve sustainable superior performance. Organizations with people who report they are more connected and engaged are also better performers across the board in a variety of measures from customer satisfaction to profitability.

An overwhelming amount of evidence points to the need to increase connection in our organizations. It is possible to thrive at work and be a catalyst for positive change. If you are ready to experience work and life at its best and are tired of settling for less, it's time to get fired up!

PART I

What Fires Us Up?

In Part I you will learn . . .

- why a sense of emotional connection is necessary for people and organizations to thrive.
- why you need connection to achieve your personal potential and how connection affects your physical and mental health.
- about research from sociologists, psychologists, and neuroscientists that increasingly demonstrates the powerful effect of connection on people.
- what elements are necessary to create a connection culture (a culture that increases connection among people).
- about the stories of two leaders and the cultures they created as illustrations of what a connection culture is and what it is not.
- about the basic human psychological needs that are met by connection and some developments in modern organizations that have become obstacles to meeting these needs for most people.

CHAPTER 1

The Case for Connection at Work

One of the most powerful and least understood aspects of business is how a sense of connection among people affects their success in life. Just as the wind moves trees and gravity moves objects, connection is invisible, yet has a very real effect on the behavior of people. I'm convinced that unless the people in an organization have a strong sense of connection—a bond that promotes trust, cooperation, and esprit de corps—they will never reach their potential as individuals, and the organization will never reach its potential.

Employees in an organization with a high degree of connection are more engaged, more productive in their jobs, and less likely to leave the organization for a competitor. Such employees are more trusting and more cooperative, share information with their colleagues, and therefore help decision makers reach well-informed decisions. Organizations that cultivate connection will be more innovative. Connection transforms a dog-eat-dog environment into a sled dog team that pulls together.[1]

So what is connection anyway? When we interact with people, we generally feel that we connect with some and not with others.

Connection describes something intangible in relationships. When it is present, we feel energy, empathy, and affirmation; when it is absent, we experience neutral or even negative feelings. Although we know what it's like to feel connected on a personal level, few among us understand the effect of connection on us and on our organizations.

Today's Widespread Disconnection and Disengagement at Work

The Gallup Organization has done extensive research in this area. The best measure of connection is Gallup's Q12 survey that asks questions about whether other people in your workplace care for you, help you grow, and consider your opinions and ideas. In 2002 the Gallup Organization published the results of a landmark research study in the *Journal of Applied Psychology* that tracked nearly eight thousand American-based business units over seven years. Business units with higher Q12 scores—in other words, higher connection—experienced higher productivity, higher profitability, and higher customer satisfaction, as well as lower employee turnover and fewer accidents.[2]

Other studies confirm the opportunity exists to improve performance by improving employee engagement. The 2004 study by the Corporate Executive Board that I mentioned earlier concluded that the most committed employees outperform the average employee by 20 percent and are 87 percent less likely to leave the organization.[3] A Hewitt study of fifteen hundred companies over four years showed companies with higher employee engagement realized higher total shareholder return.[4]

Unfortunately, Gallup research also clearly shows that the lack of connection has resulted in widespread employee disengagement. Results from its Q12 survey consistently indicate approximately 75 percent of workers do not feel engaged or connected at work.[5] The 2004 Corporate Executive Board global study of employee engagement revealed even more dismal results: 76 percent of those surveyed had a moderate commitment to their employers, and 13 percent had very little commitment.[6]

The state of many organizations today is like that of a body builder who exercises only one arm. The result: one bulging bicep and three skinny, underdeveloped limbs. Can any body builder or organization perform at its peak with only 25 percent of its members engaged?

EMPLOYEE DISENGAGEMENT IS A PROBLEM

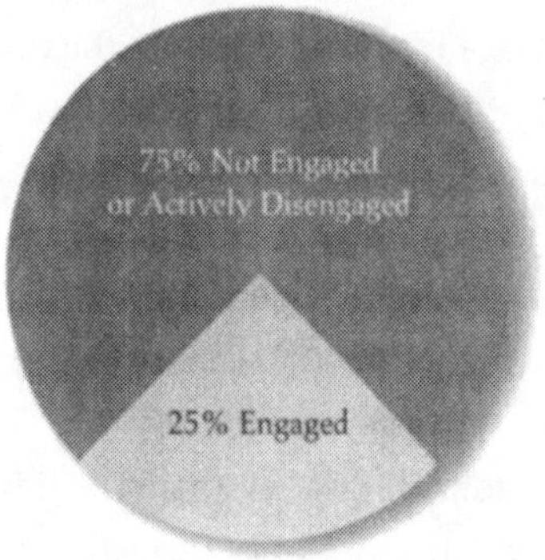

The Gallup Organization conservatively estimates the annual economic cost to the American economy from the approximately 22 million American workers who are extremely negative or "actively disengaged" to be between $250 and $300 billion. This figure doesn't include the cost for employees who are disengaged but have not spiraled down to the level of active disengagement.[7]

Widespread disengagement is a waste of human talent and energy. It's not healthy for employees or employers. People don't live with this level of frustration forever. When they are able to, many will flee to greener pastures, most likely to leaders and environments that will provide the connection they need, whether to somewhere else in your organization or to your competitor.

The Urgency of Connection

Two megatrends promise to make connection even more important: the coming labor shortage and increasing globalization of labor. In the Americas, Europe, and Asia, birth rates have plummeted below worker replacement levels.[8] When more baby boomers retire in a few years, shortages are likely in many segments of the labor market. The numbers are daunting. The US Bureau of Labor Statistics projects a shortfall of 10 million workers by 2010.[9] The Employment Policy Foundation projects a shortage of workers within this decade and lasting through much of the first half of this century. At its peak, it is expected that America will experience a shortfall of 35 million workers.[10] Because workers will have so many jobs to choose from, leaders must understand the impact of the looming labor shortage. They will need to provide a workplace culture that attracts and retains employees or suffer as insufficient labor is available to meet their growth goals.

The coming labor shortage was highlighted in a lead article of the *Harvard Business Review*. In "It's Time to Retire Retirement," authors Ken Dychtwald, Tamara Erickson, and Bob Morison concluded, after a year-long study of the implications for businesses of the aging workforce:

- Mass retirement threatens to drain talent from businesses over the next ten to fifteen years.
- Businesses will need to attract and retain older workers to meet their human resource needs.
- The workplace environment will need to be altered in order to attract and retain workers.[11]

The media's coverage of this megatrend has just begun. The *Wall Street Journal, Time, Foreign Affairs,* the *New York Times,* and other thought-leading periodicals have recently featured articles on the approaching labor shortage. You can be sure that the noise level will rise to a clamor over the years ahead.

The second megatrend, the globalization of labor, will also intensify the need to engage people at work. Many areas of the economy, such as the financial capital markets, already operate in a global manner. Financial capital easily moves around the world, and the prices of financial assets in one part of the world affect prices everywhere else. Globalization is beginning to happen with labor too.

With the rise of offshoring, globalization will continue in the market for people (or human capital, as economists describe us). Technological advances such as broadband Internet connections and online collaboration capabilities have made it easier for companies to move work and jobs around the globe. China and India have already attracted a large number of jobs from other countries. As this trend accelerates, companies that want to retain jobs in their home countries will need to boost the productivity of their people or lose business to competitors that reduce prices by offshoring.

Many firms will be unprepared for the storms ahead, however. Sydney Finkelstein of Dartmouth's Tuck School of Business studied cases of business failure to identify what managers can learn from mistakes of the past, and he noted that they usually knew of the developments in their industry that produced unfavorable change but failed to do anything about them.[12] The emerging storms from disengagement, an aging population, and globalization could turn out to be issues managers were aware of but failed to act upon. To gain a performance advantage and reduce their vulnerability in the face of these issues, leaders can intentionally create a work environment that increases engagement and connection within the organization. The reward? A business that achieves sustainable peak performance including employees who are so committed to their organization that they recruit on its behalf. It can happen and will happen when you get connected and get fired up.

Review, Reflection, and Application

- ❑ Connection affects our success in life. How is the level of connection in your life? How connected do you feel to your colleagues and to the organization where you are employed? Gallup research shows approximately three-fourths of Americans are not connected or engaged at work.

- ❑ Gallup research also shows that business units with higher levels of engagement—in other words, a higher degree of connection—experience higher productivity, higher profitability, and higher customer satisfaction, as well as lower employee turnover and accidents.

- ❑ Connection in the workplace will become even more important given the coming labor shortage and increasing globalization of labor.

- ❑ So what? Increasing connection in the workplace is a significant opportunity to improve the performance of individuals and organizations.

CHAPTER 2

The Science of Connection

In recent years, neuroscientists have discovered that positive human contact has a physiological effect on people. More specifically, it reduces the blood levels of the stress hormones epinephrine, norepinephrine, and cortisol. It increases the neurotransmitter dopamine, which enhances attention and pleasure, and serotonin, which eases fear and worry. Connection also increases the levels of oxytocin and/or vasopressin that make us more trusting and helps us bond with others.[1] In laymen's terms, connection makes us feel good. Connection provides a sense of well-being, it minimizes stress, and it makes us more trusting.

The observations of psychiatrists confirm these discoveries about connection. Dr. Edward Hallowell, a practicing psychiatrist and instructor of psychiatry at Harvard Medical School, has written that most business executives he encounters in his practice are deprived of connection with others, and he has stated that it makes them feel lonely, isolated, and confused at work. He believes that people in organizations with a deficiency of connection become distrusting, disrespectful, and dissatisfied. He describes these cultures without connection as "corrosive." To treat patients suffering from emotional isolation, Dr. Hallowell helps them increase connection in their lives.

Some psychoanalysts and psychologists at Wellesley College are doing work in what they refer to as "Relational-Cultural Theory." Based on years of research, they believe the lack of connection in the workplace is one reason why more and more mid-career women are walking away from successful careers. They sense that their workplace cultures are unhealthy. Because women in general tend to be more relational than men, they typically sense when the relational dynamics are less than ideal. Men seem to be less sensitive to connection and the damage done to individuals and organizations when connections are lacking or absent.[2]

Connection Meets Basic Human Psychological Needs

Other research establishes that connection improves mental and physical health throughout our lives[3]:

- Babies who are held, stroked, and cuddled are mentally and physically healthier.
- Adolescents who feel connected at home and at school are more well-adjusted.
- Patients with greater social support recover faster.
- People who experience positive human contact are more creative and better problem solvers.[4]

- Adults with more social relationships are less prone to sickness, depression, and suicide.
- Seniors with greater social relationships live longer.

All of this evidence begs the question, what is it about connection that makes it so powerful? We have deeply felt human needs to be respected, to be recognized for our talents, to belong, to have autonomy or control over our work, to experience personal growth, and to do work that we feel has meaning and do it in a way that we feel is ethical. When we work in an environment that recognizes these realities of our human nature, we thrive. We feel more energetic, more optimistic, and more fully alive. When we work in an environment that fails to recognize these parts of our human nature, our physical and mental health are damaged.[5]

People want and need to be valued. Psychologist Abraham Maslow, in the landmark article "A Theory of Human Motivation," described it this way:

> All people in our society (with a few pathological exceptions) have a need or desire for a stable, firmly based, (usually) high evaluation of themselves, for self-respect, or self-esteem, and for the esteem of others. By firmly based self-esteem, we mean that which is soundly based on real capacity, achievement and respect of others. These are, first, the desire for strength, for achievement, for adequacy, for confidence in the face of the world, and for independence and freedom. Secondly, we have what we may call the desire for reputation or prestige (defining it as respect or esteem from other people), recognition, attention, importance or appreciation . . . More and more today . . . there is appearing widespread appreciation of their central importance.[6]

Maslow went on to recognize that the needs for self-esteem and the esteem of others are deficit needs (needs that, if unmet over time, will produce pain and the desire to relieve them). One example of a deficit need is the physical need for nourishment. Left unmet, this deficit need produces the pain of hunger and the drive to seek food and eat.

When people are shown respect in the workplace and their real talents and contributions are genuinely recognized, they become fired up. They put their hearts into their work. Being consistently disrespected or ignored damages their sense of self-worth and drives them to seek ways to restore their status. If they are unable to, they eventually become disengaged.

Having established our need to be valued as a deficit need, Maslow commented on the effect of meeting esteem needs:

> Satisfaction of the self-esteem need leads to feelings of self-confidence, worth, strength, capability and adequacy of being useful and necessary in the world. But the thwarting of these needs produces feelings of inferiority, of weakness and of helplessness. These feelings in turn give rise to either basic self-discouragement or else neurotic trends.[7]

While Abraham Maslow brought new insights to help us understand human motivation, the individual's need to be valued has been recognized by wise observers of human nature since ancient times. The philosopher Aristotle, in his *Nicomachean Ethics*, recognized that people seek happiness, which comes, in part, from having self-esteem and receiving the honor of others that one rightly deserves. In his other works, Aristotle argued that the best state—or culture, for our purposes—is one that does everything possible to promote the pursuit of happiness.

He observed that happiness was necessary to achieve human health, vitality, and vigor, all of which are sure signs of human connection.

The human hunger for respect and recognition is strong. Left unmet, it produces lackadaisical or potentially destructive behavior. Television shows such as *The Office,* movies such as *Office Space,* and comic strips such as *Dilbert* tap into the very real discontent created when people feel they are not valued. Companies that ignore the esteem needs of their employees are committing self-sabotage. Predictably, large numbers of their employees just go through the motions, or worse, they seek ways to retaliate against an organization that marginalizes them. Unethical behavior is more likely to occur in cultures where large numbers of people are disconnected. People may be more willing to commit illegitimate acts to achieve the results they desire and win the recognition they crave or to retaliate against people who they feel treat them unfairly. Other basic human psychological needs include the needs for autonomy, personal growth, and meaning (we'll explore these needs in more detail later on).

Let's consider how the human psychological needs and connection play out in the workplace. When we first meet people, we expect them to respect us. If they look down on us or they are uncivil or condescending, we get upset. In time, as our colleagues get to know us, we expect them to appreciate or recognize us for our talents and contributions. That really makes us feel good. Later on, we expect to be treated and thought of as integral parts of the community. Our connection to the group is further strengthened when we feel we have control over our work. Connection is diminished, however, when we feel others are micromanaging or overcontrolling us. People who overcontrol us send the message that we are incompetent and that we are not trusted or respected.

Connection is enhanced when we experience personal growth. In other words, our role, our work in the group, is a good fit with our skills and provides enough challenge that we feel good when we rise to meet it but not so much that we become totally stressed out. When we are in the right role and therefore more productive, people notice and affirm us. This also increases our sense of connection to the group. Finally, we are motivated when we know our work is meaningful in some way and we are around other people who share our belief that our work is important. To the extent that these human needs for respect, recognition, belonging, autonomy, personal growth, and meaning are met, we feel connected to the group.

The bottom line is that connection plays a critical part in improving individual performance. People who are more connected with others fare better than those who are less connected. Because it meets our human needs, connection makes people more trusting, more cooperative, more empathetic, more enthusiastic, more optimistic, more energetic, more creative, and better problem solvers. In this environment, people want to help their colleagues. They are more open and share information that helps decision makers become better informed. The openness and marketplace of ideas that emerge in a trusting, cooperative environment also make people more innovative.

Review, Reflection, and Application

- ❑ Neuroscientists have shown that connection enhances attention, a sense of pleasure and trust in others, and reduces fear and worry.

- ❑ Psychiatrists have observed in business executives that their lack of connection makes them feel lonely, isolated, and confused, and makes them distrusting, disrespectful, and dissatisfied.

- ❑ Sociologists and medical researchers have discovered that from the time of our birth, people with a higher degree of connection experience superior physical and mental health.

- ❑ Connection with others has a positive effect on us because it meets our basic human psychological needs for respect, recognition, belonging, autonomy, personal growth, and meaning.

- ❑ So what? The findings of neuroscientists, psychiatrists, sociologists, and medical researchers support that a higher degree of connection improves our mental and physical performance. We ignore it at our peril.

CHAPTER 3

THE CONNECTION CULTURE

If connection is so beneficial to firing up people and to improving an organization's performance, what can be done to foster it and make it part of your organization's DNA? I believe the answer is to intentionally create a *connection culture. Culture* is the predominant beliefs and behaviors shared by a group of people. A *connection culture,* therefore, is a culture that embraces the necessary beliefs and behaviors that enhance connection among people and meet the universal human needs. The elements in a connection culture that meet these basic human psychological needs can be summarized as *vision, value,* and *voice.*

CONNECTION CULTURE ELEMENT #1: VISION

The first element of a connection culture is vision. It exists in an organization when everyone is

motivated by the organization's mission,
united by its values, and
proud of its reputation.

Sharing a purpose or set of beliefs unites and motivates people. At Memorial Sloan-Kettering Cancer Center people are united and motivated by the aspiration stated in their tagline, *the best cancer care, anywhere,* and the organization's reputation as a leading cancer center in the world.

Another example of vision is Apple Computer's "Think Different" advertising campaign. It was conceived following Steve Jobs's return to Apple in 1996 after a twelve-year exile. As you may recall, Apple had booted Jobs and brought in marketing pro John Scully to take Apple to the next level, which never happened. So the board of directors turned back to Jobs for help. One of his first efforts when he returned was to work with Apple's ad agency to create the "Think Different" campaign. It featured pictures of innovators in science, philosophy, and the arts such as theoretical physicist Albert Einstein, humanitarian Mahatma Gandhi, dancer/choreographer Martha Graham, photographer Ansel Adams, physicist Richard Feynman, and painter Pablo Picasso. The campaign communicated that Apple people were more than technologists; they were innovators and artists who gave others like themselves the tools to change the world. It created a powerful emotional bond, a connection between Jobs, Apple employees, and Apple customers, who are, by the way, intensely loyal and evangelistic when it comes to spreading the gospel of Apple.[1]

Other organizations have a compelling vision that unites and motivates their people. Charles Schwab's vision is to create "the most useful and ethical financial products in the world." Disney's vision is to "make people happy." Our vision at E Pluribus Partners is to "unlock human and corporate potential."

Another favorite example of a brilliant leader who brought vision to a group of people goes back a few years. During World War II, President Franklin Delano Roosevelt traveled to Seattle,

Washington, to meet with 18,000 aircraft workers at Boeing Corporation. FDR brought with him a young airplane pilot named Hewitt Wheless from Texas. The pilot had escaped death thanks to the resilience of the bullet-riddled B-17 plane he flew out of harm's way. His plane had been built at that very Boeing plant. Do you think seeing and hearing that young pilot thank them for saving his life connected them to a common cause? You bet it did. It transformed those welders and riveters into freedom fighters. From 1941 until 1945 American aircraft companies out-produced the Nazis three to one and built nearly three hundred thousand airplanes.[2]

Connection Culture Element #2: Value

The second element of a connection culture is value. Value exists in an organization when everyone

> *understands* the basic psychological needs of people,
> *appreciates* their positive, unique contributions, and
> *helps* them achieve their potential.

Let me give you a few examples of value in a culture. David Neeleman, the CEO of jetBlue, meets 95 percent of new employees on their first day of work. From day one he demonstrates that he values them. He also sets aside one day each week to travel on jetBlue flights where he serves beverages and gets down on his hands and knees to clean planes. His actions show that he doesn't devalue the work done by the people with the least prestigious jobs at jetBlue. Throughout the course of each day the high-energy and outgoing Neeleman is constantly connecting with crew members and customers. He knows that connection is important. In fact, he has said that most airlines treat passengers like cattle and that jetBlue is different because its crew members make personal connections with passengers. Neeleman's efforts have paid off as jetBlue's reputation as a great place to work has spread. In 2002, when jetBlue had to fill two thousand positions, it received 130,000 applications.[3] Could your organization find the best of the best if it had an application pool like that?

Value also includes protecting people from the abuse of power, such as incivility, sexual misconduct or prejudice, and other actions that make people feel disconnected from their community because it failed to protect them. On a few rare occasions, Jack Mitchell, CEO of the retail clothier Mitchells/Richards/Marshs, has told customers to take their business elsewhere because they became verbally abusive to an employee.[4]

Allan Loren, who led the turnaround of Dun and Bradstreet, established a rule that no meeting would be scheduled on Mondays or Fridays if it required people to travel over the weekend. He valued employees enough to protect their personal time. Loren also wanted to see them grow, so he matched everyone in the organization with a buddy who would provide continuous feedback about personal growth goals. Buddies were selected based on their strengths in areas in which a particular employee wanted to improve. Loren asked that employee satisfaction surveys be completed twice each year to see how people were doing.[5]

Carl Sewell, CEO of Sewell Automotive in Dallas, one of the most successful automobile retailers nationwide, intentionally hires caring people and nurtures a caring culture that creates connection among employees and customers. His passion for hiring such employees intensified after he was treated for cancer by dedicated health-care professionals at M. D. Anderson Cancer Center in Houston.[6] Sewell knows firsthand how uplifting it is to be around others who really value us.

CONNECTION CULTURE ELEMENT #3: VOICE

The third element of a connection culture is voice. It exists in an organization when everyone

seeks the ideas of others,
shares ideas and opinions honestly, and
safeguards relational connections.

Seeking and considering people's ideas and opinions help meet the human needs for respect, recognition, and belonging. "Being in the loop," so to speak, makes people feel connected to their colleagues, just as "being out of the loop" makes people feel disconnected. Voice also requires communicating in a way that is sensitive to the emotions of others. Being sensitive to people's feelings safeguards connections just as insensitivity quickly destroys them.

A. G. Lafley, the CEO of Procter & Gamble, is a master of using voice to boost the performance of his organization. Lafley actively seeks people's views. When he meets with people, he tells them what's honestly on his mind before he asks them to share the issues they are thinking about. He encourages them to "get the moose out of the closets" before they grow into bigger problems. When he first became CEO, Lafley asked P&G's chief marketing officer to conduct a survey of employees and request their ideas, many of which he ended up implementing. Lafley knows how much it fires up people to see their ideas come to life. In his interactions with people, he makes it all about them rather than all about him. And the results he has helped produce have been stunning. When he became CEO, P&G was performing poorly and morale was low. In his first twelve months, Lafley led an effort that resulted in a substantial increase in employee approval of P&G's leadership and soaring profitability and stock price, so much so that P&G was able to acquire the Gillette Corporation.[7]

THE CONNECTION FORMULA

A good way to remember the elements in a connection culture is to remember the following formula: *Vision + Value + Voice = Connection.* When these elements of a connection culture are in place, it's a win-win for individuals and organizations.

The following diagram maps the rationale that supports connection: the connection culture meets basic human psychological needs that help individuals and organizations thrive.

THE CONNECTION THRIVE CHAIN

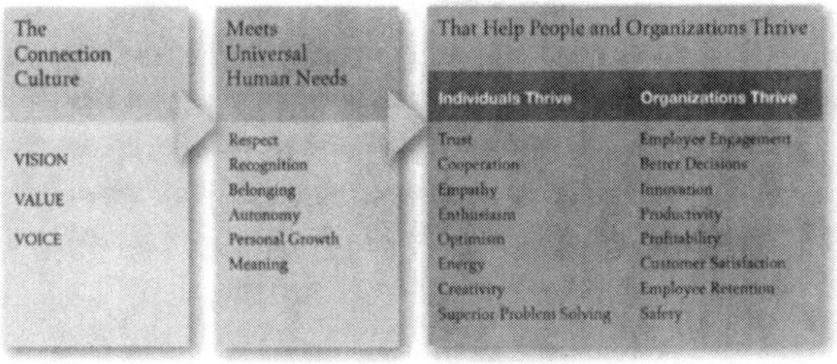

The Connection Culture
VISION
VALUE
VOICE
Meets Universal Human Needs
Respect
Recognition
Belonging
Autonomy
Personal Growth
Meaning
That Help People and Organizations Thrive
Individuals Thrive
Trust
Cooperation
Empathy
Enthusiasm
Optimism
Energy
Creativity
Superior Problem Solving
Organizations Thrive
Employee Engagement
Better Decisions
Innovation
Productivity
Profitability
Customer Satisfaction
Employee Retention
Safety

In the next two chapters, we will examine two leaders and the cultures they created to illustrate what a connection culture is and what it is not. The first leader is enshrined in the Basketball Hall of Fame where his biography credits him for producing "teams that scaled unprecedented heights that no future organization in any sport is likely to approach." The second leader produced spectacular results for a short time until the culture he created came back to haunt him.

Review, Reflection, and Application

- ❑ A connection culture is an environment that meets our basic psychological needs for respect, recognition, belonging, autonomy, personal growth, and meaning.
- ❑ The elements of a connection culture are vision, value, and voice.
- ❑ Vision exists in an organization when everyone is motivated by the organization's mission, united by its values, and proud of its reputation.
- ❑ Value exists in an organization when everyone understands the basic psychological needs of people, appreciates their positive, unique contributions, and helps them achieve their potential.
- ❑ Voice exists in an organization when everyone seeks the ideas of others, shares ideas and opinions honestly, and safeguards relational connections.
- ❑ The connection formula is Vision + Value + Voice = Connection.
- ❑ Have you experienced a sense of connection in some workplaces but not in others?

- ❑ As a consumer, have you experienced connection with the people who work for a company from which you purchased goods or services? Have there been times you felt a sense of connection to your fellow citizens? Consider what you can learn from your personal experiences with connection.

- ❑ So what? A connection culture increases connection among people by increasing the cultural elements of vision, value, and voice. Leaders should be intentional about creating a connection culture in order to reap its benefits.

CHAPTER 4

Connection and the Legend

So often in life, good things bloom from the seeds of hardship. The personal character of a young teenager who went on to become a great leader was immeasurably shaped during the Depression when his family lost their farm in Indiana. His father's reaction to the loss was unusual: he wasn't bitter about it. Instead, his dad focused on the future and told his children that everything would be all right. And it was.

During those impressionable years in this leader's life, he learned that, like the Depression, some things in life are not in our control. His father taught him that he should always strive to do his best at anything he chose to do and not worry about the outcome. He would later spread that philosophy to countless others.

Another perspective he gained during those formative years was to value people. By watching his mom and dad and hearing the stories of faith they taught him, he learned the joy that came from making people and relationships his focus in life.

The young boy grew up to be an outstanding high school and college basketball player in a state that was rabid about the game. After college he married Nell, the love of his life and the only woman he had ever dated. He taught high school English and coached basketball until 1943 when he enlisted to serve in the navy during World War II. When he returned from the war to the high school in South Bend, Indiana, where he previously taught, he was offered his old job. Other returning GIs were not, however, and so he refused the offer because he felt it was wrong for the school to deny veterans the jobs they had left to serve their country. Instead, he accepted an offer to become athletic director and head basketball coach at Indiana State Teachers College.[1]

A Caring Coach

For the 1946–47 season Indiana State received a postseason invitation to the National Association of Intercollegiate Basketball (NAIB) national play-offs. After the coach learned that a young African-American second-string guard on his team, Clarence Walker, would not be allowed to participate in the tournament because of the color of his skin, he declined the offer. The following season NAIB officials invited Indiana State again, and this time decided they would allow Clarence to play, provided he didn't stay at the hotel with his teammates and wouldn't be seen publicly with them. Once again the coach declined. He and Nell thought of all the young men on the team as extended members of their family whom they loved, and the coach wasn't about to allow Clarence to be humiliated. But Clarence and his family saw it in a different light. They were excited about the opportunity for him to become the first African-American player in history to participate in the prestigious tournament. So they, along with officials from the NAACP, approached the coach to persuade him that attending the tournament would help, not hurt, Clarence and other African-American players. The coach decided to accept the NAIB's offer, and the team packed up to head to the play-offs in Kansas City.

On their way to the tournament, the team bus stopped for meals. If a restaurant wouldn't serve Clarence, the coach would make the team get back on the bus. Often the team had to pick up food at grocery stores along the way and eat on the bus.

When Clarence finally walked onto the basketball court to warm up, he appeared to be nearly paralyzed with fear. Many people in the crowd spotted the courageous young man, and they began to applaud. Clarence Walker became the first African-American player to participate in the NAIB play-offs, and Indiana State made it to the finals, where they lost to Louisville. Because of Clarence's courage and his coach's resolve to stand up for what he believed in, the NAIB tournament was finally opened to African-American student-athletes. The following season three teams brought African-American players with them to the tournament.

John Robert Wooden went on to become head basketball coach of the UCLA Bruins (1948–75). His fired up teams won more than 80 percent of their games and ten national championships, and had four perfect seasons. Coach Wooden was the first person in history to be inducted twice into the Basketball Hall of Fame. In 1961, he was honored for his achievements as a player at Purdue University where he was All-American, college player of the year, and a leader of the Boilermakers' 1932 National Championship Team. In 1973, he was honored for his achievements as a coach.

In the summer of 2003, the ninety-two-year-old Wooden traveled to the White House, where he was awarded the Presidential Medal of Freedom, America's highest civilian honor.[2] In December, with many of the players Wooden coached surrounding him at the ceremony, UCLA's Pauley Pavilion was renamed the Nell and John Wooden Court.

The Secret of His Success

What was it about Wooden that produced such extraordinary success as a student-athlete and then as a coach? Bill Walton, the Hall of Fame basketball player and television sportscaster who played for the coach on two national championship teams, identified the essence of Wooden's success when he stated, "[Coach Wooden] created an environment that people wanted to be a part of."[3]

To begin with, that environment included vision. Wooden instilled a tremendous sense of pride in his players about being a part of the UCLA basketball team. He taught them, as Bill Walton wrote, "If you lived up to your responsibilities as a student and a human being, then you earned the privilege of becoming a member of the UCLA basketball team."[4] Integral to meeting his standards was achieving the character values reflected in what he called "the Pyramid of Success." The character values, or blocks of the pyramid, were industriousness, enthusiasm, friendship, loyalty, cooperation, self-control, alertness, initiative, intentness, condition, skill, and team spirit. Wooden taught his players that believing and behaving in a way consistent with these character values produced poise and confidence that resulted in competitive greatness (that is, the desire to continuously challenge oneself in life). Patience and faith make up the mortar that holds all of the blocks together. When the pyramid was built, the person met the standards that John Wooden believed made him a success and earned him the right to be called a member of the UCLA basketball team.

Wooden taught and lived out the character values he wanted his players to adopt. They had a vision to strive for as individuals and together as a team. Kareem Abdul-Jabbar, one of the greatest basketball players in history, who played his entire college career with Wooden, would later write, "Coach Wooden had a profound influence on me as an athlete, but even greater influence on me as a human being. He is responsible, in part, for the person I am today."[5] Bill Walton astutely observed that "we have become John Wooden ourselves."[6] And in a sense they did by accepting Wooden's beliefs, his character values, as their own. As Wooden worked to reproduce people who shared the values reflected in the pyramid, the UCLA basketball team became more connected to their coach and to each other.

Wooden infused the UCLA basketball team environment with value. It began with respect for everyone, regardless of a person's status on the team or in society. The way Wooden stood up for the returning GIs and Clarence Walker showed that he modeled respect for others. For much of his career Wooden worked alongside the student managers as they swept or mopped the basketball court before practices to set an example that no position was unimportant. He required even the best players to clean up after themselves in the locker room and not to expect the student managers to do it. All of his players were to be respectful toward flight attendants, waitresses and waiters, and hotel workers they encountered while traveling with the team. He always said, "You're as good as anybody, but you're no better than anybody."

Integral to Coach Wooden's view of valuing people was the notion of helping them reach their potential as basketball players and as people. Bill Walton described it this way: "You were competing against an ideal, an abstract standard of excellence defined by John Wooden. The actual opponents mattered little. It was the ideal that mattered most."[7] Wooden pushed his players to be the best they were capable of becoming, running long and demanding practices. According to Walton, before and after practice, the coach was calm, but during practice sessions Wooden "prowled the sidelines like a caged tiger . . . He never stopped moving, never stopped chattering away. Up and down the court he would pace, always barking out his pet little phrases . . . 'failing to prepare is preparing to fail . . . never mistake activity for achievement.' He liked to say, 'Make the effort. Do your best. The score cannot make you a loser when you do that; it cannot make you a winner if you do less.'"[8] If his players didn't work hard enough during practice, as hard as he did preparing for it, he ordered them off the court, then had the student managers collect the balls, turn off the lights, and lock the doors.

Coach Wooden operated a meritocracy that treated every player fairly. He didn't believe in the star system and told his players, "The star of the team is the team." Wooden benched Sidney Wicks, one of the nation's best players, for a season because he wasn't passing to his open teammates. (The following year, a more selfless Wicks was awarded All-American honors and helped UCLA win a national championship.) No one's position was safe if Wooden felt another player had proven he could perform better for the team's sake. At the same time, however, he recognized that the nonstarters didn't receive the adulation that starters did. So he encouraged and affirmed them in practice, and as he said in an interview in 1996, "I became a little closer with some of my players [who] didn't get to play very much."

Another element in the environment created by Wooden was voice. He encouraged everyone to adopt an attitude of openness to ideas and opinions. One of his favorite sayings was "when everybody thinks alike, nobody thinks." Wooden typically shared his opinions and encouraged others to share theirs before he made most decisions, unless time was of the essence, say, in the midst of a game. If asked for advice, Wooden would reply, "I don't give advice; I give opinions."

Wooden's tolerance for others' views was tested when Bill Walton wrote a protest letter about the Vietnam War on the UCLA basketball team stationery, had his teammates sign it, and asked Wooden if he would sign it too. Although the coach declined to sign, he allowed Walton to mail the letter to then President Richard Nixon.

A stark contrast to the connection culture developed by John Wooden and the UCLA basketball team is the culture described in the following story of one of the most spectacular falls of a leader in recent history.

Review, Reflection, and Application

- ❑ John Wooden, the coach with (some would say) the best record in any sport, created a culture in the UCLA basketball team that included the elements of vision, value, and voice.

- ❑ Over the course of your life thus far, who has connected with and engaged, or even inspired, you the most? You should consider your parents, coaches, teachers, instructors, and the other leaders you have come in contact with as well as your friends, teammates, and colleagues at work. Why did they have that effect on you? Were their words or deeds that affected you aspects of vision, value, or voice?

- ❑ So what? Arguably the greatest coach ever in any sport created a connection culture, John Wooden was a role model who embodied vision, value, and voice. If you are a leader, how do you compare to John Wooden? How do the leaders in your organization compare to him, and how can they improve?

CHAPTER 5

Trouble in Times Square

During the summer of 2003, Howell Raines was on top of the world. As executive editor of the *New York Times*, the fifty-nine-year-old Alabaman held one of the most powerful leadership positions in all of journalism. After the *Times* had garnered a record seven Pulitzer Prizes for its coverage of September 11, Raines stood on the floor of the newsroom at Forty-third and Broadway in the heart of Times Square and boldly proclaimed to the staff that what they did "will be studied and taught as long as journalism is . . . practiced."[1]

Within a year he was fired.

The less-than-two-year tenure of Howell Raines was the second shortest for an executive editor in the more than 150-year history of the *New York Times*. To understand what led to the fall of Howell Raines is to understand something basic about leadership and the culture leaders help create.

Raines's fall wasn't due to his failure as a newspaperman. As a reporter, he was among the best in the business, having written a long list of outstanding articles and books and having received the coveted Pulitzer Prize. And Raines was determined to be successful.

He was known as a hard-charging leader who liked to say he was raising the competitive metabolism of the *Times* newsroom. Abundant knowledge of the business and resolve were not the issue.

A Culture of Disconnection

Raines's leadership style and the culture he created in the newsroom led to his undoing. His demise accelerated with the scandal and subsequent investigation of the plagiarism and fabrication by Jayson Blair, one of Raines's young star reporters. Smelling an opportunity to get rid of Raines, *Times* reporters lined up to testify against the way he ran the newsroom. Accounts of the situation as reported in the *New Yorker* and the *Wall Street Journal* revealed the following:

- Employees viewed Raines as inaccessible and arrogant.
- Employees feared to disagree with Raines or bring him any bad news.
- Raines and his small circle of loyalists tightly controlled decision making and didn't trust department editors with decisions that normally would be theirs to make.
- Raines was perceived as unfairly applying a two-tier system that allowed stars such as Jayson Blair to skirt the rules while holding other newsroom employees to stricter reporting and editing standards.
- Policies that Raines had put in place regarding transfers and travel were so unpopular they caused talented reporters and a bureau chief to leave for other news organizations.

In short, Howell Raines played favorites, denying many people opportunities to show what they were capable of doing. He centralized decisions and was perceived as not being open to constructive criticism. The people who were not in Raines's inner circle felt deeply disconnected. Vision, value, and voice were in short supply.

It is not my intention to demonize Howell Raines. In fact, there is much to admire about him. He was awarded the Pulitzer Prize for a touching story he wrote about the positive influence of Grady Hutchinson, his family's African-American housekeeper, on him as a child growing up in Birmingham, Alabama. Ms. Hutchinson has said that her relationship with Howell Raines has been one of the highlights in her life. Raines's book on the history of the civil rights struggle shows his desire to make a positive contribution to the world. I believe that Raines, like many, suffered from being blind to the effects of his words and actions on others.

The culture that Raines created was more about power than principle. People with rank ordered others about. They learned from Raines that the powerful didn't need to consider the opinions of others; in fact, it was a sign of weakness to do so. Raines told colleagues that his father, a successful businessman, had once advised him that when an employee challenged him, he had to "win that fight." Raines created a star system where the favored few, the stars, were not held to the rigorous journalistic standards that others were required to meet.

Raines taught that power and privilege were paramount. Wooden taught that the principles of respect for others and sacrifice for the sake of your teammates and the team as a whole were the highest calling, and only by understanding and living by those values could you become a winner.

Wooden and Raines: Different Cultures . . . Different Results

The culture John Wooden created was a connection culture that fired up his team's spirits, and as a result, their performance soared! UCLA's unsurpassed record proves it. The culture Howell Raines created for those who were not in his inner circle was a culture of disconnection that was spirit numbing at best and spirit crushing at worst. Over time a culture that results in low connection or disconnection will burn out people; it's just a question of when. It's no surprise that the pent-up frustration in the *New York Times* newsroom led to a mutiny when the investigation over the Jayson Blair debacle ensued and many of the newsroom employees sensed Raines was vulnerable. As the *Wall Street Journal* reported, "In the end, Mr. Raines' demise came swiftly . . . he had few . . . allies."

Review, Reflection, and Application

- ❑ Howell Raines, former executive editor of the *New York Times,* achieved success for a while until the culture he created came back to haunt him. His words and actions made the people he considered to be stars feel connected and engaged while others felt disconnected and subsequently pounced on him when he became politically vulnerable.

- ❑ What will your legacy be with your family, your colleagues at work, and your friends and acquaintances in your community? Will you be fondly remembered as a person who fired up people, or will people revile you for wearing them down, discouraging or ignoring them?

- [ ] So what? If you are in a culture that has little connection, like the culture Howell Raines created in the *New York Times* newsroom, look for ways to increase connection, or get out and find a connection culture where you can thrive.

CHAPTER 6

THE NEXT STEP IN THE EVOLUTION OF ORGANIZATIONS

Most organizations today have become masters of *task excellence,* that is, the hard, quantitative, and analytically oriented aspects of business implicit in such areas as Six Sigma (a statistically oriented quality improvement program) and competitive benchmarking (the practice of comparing objective measures such as sales, profits, or inventory level to those of one's competitors). Unfortunately, organizations that focus on task excellence alone will fail to meet the basic human psychological needs that maximize employees' contributions to the organization.[1]

More and more leaders are beginning to see that, absent the connection and engagement that results when these needs are met, peak performance is not sustainable. With task excellence alone, success is fleeting.

People are both the problem and the solution. We need one another to accomplish great things, but we operate toward one another as if it's "all about me." The solution to this problem is to create a connection culture that will meet our psychological needs.

Star Systems on Steroids

The prevalence and extreme nature of star systems today contribute to widespread employee disconnection and disengagement. Employees can be regarded as stars, core employees, or strugglers. Stars are superior performers. They are either a part of senior management or on track to move up the organization's hierarchy. Core employees are valuable contributors but not stars. Strugglers perform poorly, some for temporary reasons and others because they may not fit well in their roles or with the company.

Star systems affect the economic, political, and social aspects of organizations. Leaders are more likely to favor stars economically by paying them more; politically by keeping them more informed, listening to and considering their points of view; and socially by spending more time with them and treating them as if they are superior human beings. Be assured, the favoritism is noticed. The star system is similar to a caste system: the stars are Brahman or gentry, strugglers are the untouchables or peasants, and core employees fall somewhere in between. This system makes most employees feel like second-class citizens.[2]

Please understand that I do not oppose linking rewards to performance. I do believe, however, that it can be carried too far not only economically—an issue that the media regularly focuses on—but also and perhaps more important, politically and socially, especially in light of the value provided by core employees.

Research by Thomas DeLong at Harvard Business School and Vineeta Vijayaraghavan of Katzenbach Partners sheds some light on categorizing employees. Their research has shown that "B players" (whom I prefer to call core employees) are just as critical, and often more so, to an organization's success as its stars. Core employees comprise the vast majority of an organization's employees. They are often just as intelligent, talented, and knowledgeable as stars, yet they differ from them in several respects:

- Core employees are less likely to call attention to themselves.
- Core employees are less likely to leave their current employers for greener pastures.
- Core employees are quietly dedicated to their work and to their teammates.

Not all core employees are alike. Some core employees are former stars who now seek greater work/life balance. Others are "go-to" players who help their colleagues navigate the organization. Still other core employees are "truth tellers" who, although blunt at times in their criticism, help assure the organization addresses important issues that others may be less willing to raise.[3]

With the prolonged state of employee disengagement and disconnection there is good reason to believe that companies are vulnerable to losing many core employees in the years ahead. The reason: core employees feel their ideas and opinions are not sought or heard, and they are not respected or recognized for their work. At some level this lack of consideration is discouraging, and over time they become frustrated. Although they know that they're valuable, feeling underappreciated keeps them from putting their hearts into their work.

Other factors contributing to the disconnection and disengagement of core employees has been the stream of high-profile cases of corporate malfeasance, several consecutive years of downsizing, and the compensation differential between the company's stars and the rest of the employees. Employee loyalty has waned; the relationship between most workers and leaders has eroded.

Whether leaders realize it or not, they are sending the message to core employees that they are second-class citizens, that shareholders and the company's stars are one team and the rest of the employees are another.

The pendulum has swung too far in the direction of the stars. Organizations need to treat everyone with dignity and respect within a meritocracy that allocates important projects to stars while giving core employees opportunities to prove that they can be stars too.

Putting the Corpus Back into Corporations

One organization that balances meritocracy with connecting and engaging core employees is the United States Marine Corps. Given its mission, the Marine Corps cannot afford to tolerate suboptimal performance from any members. To get the best performance out of everyone, the Marines have adopted inclusive practices to make all members feel like a part of the team. In the Marine Corps everyone is considered important, and all complete leadership training. With this level of expectation and respect for the contribution of all members, it should come as no surprise that in a McKinsey & Company/Conference Board study of thirty organizations known to have engaged frontline workers, the Marine Corps was cited as the best.[4]

The English word *corporation* is derived from the Latin *corpus,* which means "body." When people come together to work toward a common purpose or to accomplish a common mission, they can secure state approval to become a legal corporation. This newly created body is comprised of individuals connected to one another via the corporate relationship and each with a specific role to play as a part of the whole.

If we are to solve the problems of employee disconnection, disengagement, and burnout, as well as the societal ills flowing from them, one means will surely be to put the *corpus* back into corporations. In other words, we need to adopt the mind-set that as members of corporations, we are in community with one another, linked together so that what damages any member of the body harms everyone else and, likewise, what strengthens any member strengthens everyone else. We need to build internal relationships that create trusted colleagues rather than internal competitors. We need to channel our competitive energy toward reaching our individual and corporate potential in the same way that Coach John Wooden encouraged his players to reach their individual potential rather than focus on beating a teammate.

Let's face it, people are complicated. With a connection culture, I am not advocating having employees standing around, holding hands, and singing "Kum Ba Yah." I am not promoting a warm and fuzzy work environment or employee group therapy sessions. I know that you may not like all of your fellow workers. That said, creating a work environment that cultivates healthy self-esteem and strong working relationships is common sense, yet uncommon in practice.

Wise leaders are beginning to see the gap between what exists today and what we all long for. These leaders are ushering in a new era in the evolution of organizations. One day it will be widely acknowledged that task excellence is only part of what's necessary for organizations to achieve sustainable superior performance. People will eventually understand that the soft issues that increase connection among people are essential to any organization that aspires to be the best. It will also be recognized that star systems carried to extremes can be destructive to long-term organizational health because they sow disconnection.

Leaders and organizations that take action to increase connection will thrive. Many of those that don't will not survive as their better-connected, more-productive, and more-innovative competitors filled with fired up people pass them by. In Part II we will look more closely at the three elements in a connection culture that will drive this change.

Review, Reflection, and Application

- ❑ Task excellence is not enough. Organizations must also have the relationship excellence that results from connection to achieve sustainable superior performance.
- ❑ A star system in an organization usually results in creating a large class of marginalized core employees who are, in reality, the foundation of the organization.
- ❑ The elements in a connection culture—vision, value, and voice—work in concert to ensure that the foundational human needs are met in legitimate ways.
- ❑ Have the leaders in your organization created a culture of connection that engages people? If you are a leader, do you actively value people and seek to help them achieve their potential?
- ❑ So what? Meeting the basic human psychological needs increases connection and results in a greater level of fired up people who are more productive and more innovative. This is not a "nice to have"; it's a "must have" in any successful organization. Without it, workers will, at best, underperform and, at worst, sabotage the organization.

PART II

The Three Keys to Connecting Your Team and Lighting Their Fires:

Vision, Value, and Voice

In Part II you will learn . . .

- how the elements of vision, value, and voice are reflected in the richer concepts of inspiring identity, human value, and knowledge flow.
- what the elements of a connection culture look like in an organization through modern and historical examples.
- how to apply the elements and increase connection in organizational environments.

CHAPTER 7

INSPIRE WITH IDENTITY

In Warren Bennis and Patricia Ward Biederman's insightful book *Organizing Genius,* they tell the story of America's race to make an atomic bomb before the Nazis during World War II. The Manhattan Project, as it was called, represented one of the most challenging and significant scientific accomplishments in history.

The story began in 1939 when Albert Einstein learned from three Hungarian physicists who had defected to America that the Nazis were trying to build an atomic bomb. Einstein wrote a letter to President Franklin Delano Roosevelt warning him that he believed the Nazis might find a way to do it. Within days of receiving Einstein's letter, FDR established an advisory committee to investigate using atomic energy for national defense.

During 1941 and 1942, research was conducted at four universities: Columbia, Princeton, Berkeley, and Chicago. By mid-1942, the project had become the number-one defense priority with a $2 billion budget. In the fall, soon-to-be Brigadier General Leslie Groves was appointed to head the project following his stint building the Pentagon. Groves, a 250- to 300-pound crusty veteran career officer, began to pull together the people and the resources to make it happen.

On December 2, 1942, a team led by Enrico Fermi, a brilliant physicist, successfully created a self-sustaining nuclear reaction in an unused squash court under the University of Chicago's football stadium. It was a pivotal moment that meant the project could shift to producing an atomic bomb since the concept had been proven.

General Groves identified a tall, gangly thirty-eight-year-old quantum physicist at Cal Tech, J. Robert Oppenheimer, to be the technical leader of the scientists and engineers. Although military intelligence officials objected to Oppenheimer because of his Communist Party connections, General Groves insisted that he was the best person for the job. Refusing to back down, the persistent Groves got Oppenheimer approved.[1]

One scientist on the project was a young genius from Princeton named Richard Feynman who was to supervise technicians supporting the project. For security reasons, the army did not want the technicians to know the purpose of the project. As a result, it was difficult for them to put their hearts into their work. Their productivity was lackluster, and the quality of their work was disappointing. Feynman asked Oppenheimer to let him inform the technicians about the project's purpose. His request approved, Feynman explained to the technicians what they were working on, its importance to the war effort, and the value of their contribution to the overall project.

After the technicians understood the meaning of their work, Feynman said he witnessed:

> Complete transformation! They began to invent ways of doing it better. They improved the scheme. They worked at night. They didn't need supervising in the night; they didn't need

> anything. They understood everything; they invented several of the programs that we used . . . my boys really came through, and all that had to be done was to tell them what it was, that's all. As a result, although it took them nine months to do three problems before, we did nine problems in three months, which is nearly ten times as fast.[2]

The technicians' improved productivity and innovation helped the Allies beat Hitler in the race to make an atomic bomb. On the morning of July 16, 1945, the Manhattan Project team watched as the first atomic bomb was exploded in the New Mexico desert. Their efforts gave the Allies a decisive edge in the war. Regardless of your personal feelings about the development and use of the atomic bomb, this bit of history is one clear example of the power in helping people find meaning in their work.

The Organization's Story Is My Story Too

Each one of us has a personal identity, in other words, how we think about ourselves. This internal identity is shaped by a host of factors, such as where we grew up, how we were raised, the schools we attended, and the people and events in our lives that influenced our beliefs and our aspirations. Our identities are expressed externally in where we work, what organizations we belong to (other than work), what we wear, what we drive, where we live, and so on. Identity influences almost everything we do. Savvy marketers understand this and shape brands to appeal to how we like to think of ourselves.

Organizations have identities too. I like to think of identity as the story of an individual or organization. Some stories, such as those of the Marine Corps, Memorial Sloan-Kettering Cancer Center, and Apple Computer, provide tremendous inspiration to the people who are a part of them and who, through their words and deeds, continue to write new chapters in the identity story of their organizations.

Part I introduced the terms *vision, value,* and *voice* as an easy way to remember the elements in a connection culture. As we dig deeper into each element, I want to expand the terms to capture the full breadth and depth of their significance.

Vision represents the cultural element of *inspiring identity.* To be effective here, it's necessary to go beyond task thinking and transform the way people think about the organization. The inspiring identity of an organization helps to satisfy the sense of purpose, significance, and pride we all crave. It bears repeating that unless you inspire people, you have not added this element to the work environment. And absent inspiration that fires them up, people just show up for duty.

We Band of Brothers

In 1415 King Henry V of England led thirteen thousand of his men in battle against fifty thousand Frenchmen near the village of Agincourt in northern France. The young king came to France because he felt that the French were controlling territory that rightfully belonged to him. Henry and his small army were there to take it back. And that's exactly what they did. Although heavily outnumbered by nearly four to one, Henry and his men routed the French forces in one of the greatest battles in English history.

Historian Simon Schama described Henry as "the dark-haired, pale-faced, unnervingly sober king . . . St. George and a

Galahad wrapped up in one unbeatable package."[3] No doubt about it, Henry was one capable king on a mission. But how did he motivate the Englishmen to follow him into a battle when they were so overwhelmingly outnumbered? William Shakespeare was fascinated by this question, too, and he wrote about it in the play *Henry V* that immortalized Henry and the battle at Agincourt.

According to Shakespeare's account, Henry's troops had their doubts as they looked upon the heavily armored, highly skilled French lords and knights. King Henry had to do something to give his troops the resolve to fight and win in the face of enormous odds against them. As the battle was about to begin, Henry overheard some fellow Englishmen wishing they could be back in England rather than fighting the French. Knowing that he needed to get the best out of his men, he decided to address them. He began by questioning why anyone would want to miss out on the victory ahead. He then promised anyone who joined with him that

> . . . we in it shall be remember'd,
> We few, we happy few, we band of brothers;
> For he to-day that sheds his blood with me
> Shall be my brother; be he ne'er so vile,
> This day shall gentle his condition:
> And gentlemen in England now a-bed
> Shall think themselves accursed they were not here,
> And hold their manhoods cheap whiles any speaks
> That fought with us upon Saint Crispin's day.[4]

Henry knew, or at least Shakespeare thought he did, that appealing to the men's desire for recognition, respect, and meaning in their lives was the key to unleashing their energy. Promising that anyone who fought alongside him in this glorious battle would be considered, in a sense, one of Henry's "band of brothers," regardless of how lowly or "vile" a particular soldier was, was heady stuff for men who believed that they were born into their stations in life and that the young Henry was appointed by God to rule England. By fighting alongside Henry, these soldiers believed they were becoming part of a relatively small number of men who would always be looked up to for their amazing victory. It gave them something to be proud of. It would make "somebodies" out of nobodies by transforming their identities.

Helping people to achieve the respectable status that they crave is a powerful motivator. King Henry V elevated those who fought with him from their lowly positions in society, a stigma that made them feel devalued. By restoring their sense of value and elevating their status, their identity, Henry tapped into a way of engaging and energizing his soldiers. King Henry V was so successful that by the time of his death from disease seven years later, he had taken control of half of France.

Meaning Matters

Instilling a sense of purpose in the minds of people can transform them. Dr. Viktor Frankl, the great Viennese psychiatrist and Holocaust survivor, wrote in his seminal work *Man's Search for Meaning* that the survivors of concentration camps looked to the future and found meaning in their lives. Without meaning, people feel empty and apathetic. Frankl explained that most people find meaning in work or love.[5] For the technicians working on the Manhattan Project, knowing the importance of their work motivated them, and their productivity increased tenfold. For the soldiers fighting alongside King Henry V, their victory at

Agincourt assured them a meaningful position in medieval society. In the next chapter we will consider several ways to bring meaning to work.

Review, Reflection, and Application

- ❑ Inspiring identity exists in an organization when everyone is motivated by the organization's mission, united by its values, and proud of its reputation. Individuals have stories about their identities that influence them. Organizations have identity stories that influence individuals too.

- ❑ After physicist Richard Feynman explained the meaning of the Manhattan Project to the supporting engineers (that they were racing against the Nazis to build a nuclear bomb), their productivity increased nearly tenfold.

- ❑ According to Shakespeare, King Henry V defeated the French at Agincourt in part because he inspired his soldiers to think of how proud they would be when they returned to England as victors in this historic battle. He gave them an inspiring identity.

- ❑ According to psychiatrist Viktor Frankl, most people find meaning in work or love. In your workplace, how do people find meaning in their work?

- ❑ So what? Leaders need to bring meaning to their organizations because an individual's work is an important part of his personal identity.

CHAPTER 8

CREATE MEANING IN YOUR ORGANIZATION

Well, you might be thinking, *it's easy to find meaning when you are racing to save the civilized world from Hitler, but how can I provide meaning to employees who are making electric motors or providing financial services?* Although it's not as obvious, it is achievable. Let me identify a few ways in which leaders can provide meaning and significance to the work of the people they lead.

1. *Be an innovator.* One way to find meaning in work is to show how you are bringing something new or different to the marketplace. Harvard Business School's Michael Porter put it this way: "In great companies, strategy becomes a cause. That's because strategy is about being different. So if you have a really great strategy, people are fired up: 'We're not just another airline. We're bringing something new to the world.'"[1]

In his humorous and fascinating book *On Paradise Drive*, astute social critic David Brooks observed this about people who have a vision to bring something new to the market:

> The press concentrates its attention on the remarkable figures, the dot-com geniuses, the zillionaire investment bankers, or the paradigm-shifting, over-the-horizon-peering, outside-the-box-thinking corporate rebels who let their wacky but brilliant employees scooter down the company hallways while squirting each other with Super Soaker water cannons. But the real engines of American capitalism are the people you see in the most unremarkable locales—sitting around in the bland office parks or checking in to the suite hotels . . .
>
> Perhaps one of the people . . . dreams of revolutionizing supermarket razor displays . . . Maybe others spend their days thinking about how to reduce glare on cash register displays so that older employees can read them better; or perhaps they obsess over how to speed up the receipt printer so that supermarket lines can move a tiny bit faster . . . These are the drivers of the American economy.[2]

Brooks goes on to explain how many individuals are driven by what he refers to as a "Paradise Spell," a vision of a better future that propels them to work hard so that they might achieve it. It is another way of saying that these driven individuals are motivated to bring something new to the world. Being an innovator is part of their personal story, part of their identity. Do the members in your organization feel like innovators?

2. *Inspire your team to reach a challenging goal.* Another way to fire up the spirit of healthy competition and bring meaning to work is to give people a challenge or set a goal to be the best organization in your business at some measure such as revenue, profit, or client satisfaction. This works especially well if you have access to benchmarking information that lets you see how your

organization's performance compares to your competitors'. Being the leader of something enhances a person's identity.

Often leaders try to create internal competition among individuals within a unit. Although internal competition may motivate employees, it also destroys trust and cooperation. You don't want individuals in a unit to perceive each other as competitors rather than colleagues, especially if successful performance requires a high degree of teamwork. You want them to focus energy on external competitors or on individual best efforts. Coach John Wooden told his basketball players that success is the peace of mind that comes from knowing you gave your very best effort in every practice and every game rather than focusing on anything outside your control. As a result, Wooden's players relentlessly pushed themselves to live up to their own personal standards.

In an effort to "stir the pot," some leaders make individual performance results available for all to see, thus shaming individuals with poor performance. A better approach is to use performance measures as benchmarks to identify whether individuals are in the right role or have performance issues that can be corrected. I do not mean just looking at quarterly data, however, but taking into account a longer time frame. Everyone experiences slumps for one reason or another, and examining only a short period of time is myopic.

Shaming someone by making his performance numbers public violates the element of *human value* (we will discuss it in later chapters). If a person is not performing after attempts have been made to help him, it is best to reevaluate the individual's skills, temperament, and so forth and make every effort to move him into the appropriate role. If one doesn't exist, assist him with a severance and outplacement package that eases his transition to another organization. People in your company will see that you treated the underperformer with dignity and respect, and your organization will be more appealing to the remaining employees.

3. *Communicate your inspiring identity upfront.* New employee orientation often consists of merely a member from each department briefly explaining the department's activities along with a review of who's who. Great leaders take the time to invest in new employees upfront so that they may understand the organization, its meaning, and their role in it. Educating new members begins with a well-planned orientation program. The more thorough understanding people have of their organization, the more they will feel connected.

As I mentioned earlier, in the mid-to late-1990s, McKinsey & Company and The Conference Board jointly studied thirty organizations known to have engaged frontline workers, and the project team concluded the United States Marine Corps outperformed all other organizations in motivating its frontline members. One of the best practices of the Corps is inculcating the meaning of its work to new recruits during the twelve-week boot camp at Parris Island, South Carolina. The Marines' best leaders teach recruits the values of honor, courage, and commitment.

During boot camp, recruits learn the words and meaning of the "Marines' Hymn," including these key phrases: "we fight our country's battles," "first to fight for right and freedom," "we have fought in every clime and place where we could take a gun," and "in many a strife, we've fought for life." The recruits are not called *Marines* until they have successfully completed the portion of the boot camp called *The Crucible.* Various stages of The Crucible include evaluations that are named after Medal of Honor recipients. Recruits learn the stories of Medal of Honor recipients such as Daniel Daly.

During World War I at Belleau Wood in France, Daly—armed with hand grenades and a pistol—single-handedly attacked and defeated an enemy machine gun emplacement. Later that same day and while under enemy attack, Daly brought in wounded from the battlefield. He would have been awarded the Medal of Honor, but he already had been awarded two others—the maximum allowed.[3]

With upfront orientation that includes other similar stories, it should be no surprise that when you ask a Marine what's so special about the Marine Corps, he or she will reply, *esprit de corps*, a French phrase meaning the "spirit of the group." The Corps' spirit is the foundation that produces a lifelong commitment reflected in the Marine Corps' motto, *Semper Fidelis* (Latin for "always faithful").

4. *Consistently communicate your inspiring identity.* Every leader should aspire not only to create but also to sustain an organization and environment where everyone is united by a common desire to be "always faithful" to the organization's vision and its members. We all long to be part of an organization that is worthy of our heartfelt, sincere commitment. Corporate leaders need to see themselves as chief spiritual officers, if you will, in the sense that they are responsible for creating and sustaining the conditions that foster employee commitment and infusing their team with a desire to achieve the mission. They can do this by continuously spreading the vision, mission, and values of the organization and linking in the minds of employees the company's inspiring identity to its current situation, tactical action plans, and strategy. Abraham Lincoln, FDR, and Winston Churchill were just a few of the great leaders who kept an inspiring identity in front of the people and called upon them to put forth the extra effort to accomplish their common goal.

5. *Employ the power of the pen.* Historically, great leaders have used public speaking and writing to persuade people and influence their behavior. Thomas Paine's pamphlet *Common Sense* had a tremendous effect on starting the American Revolution, as did Patrick Henry's "give me liberty or give me death" speech. Martin Luther King Jr.'s "I Have a Dream" speech and "Letter from Birmingham Jail" are perhaps two of the most important pieces of persuasive communications that contributed to the passage of the Civil Rights Act of 1964.

In the world of business, *Pour Your Heart into It* by Howard Schultz of Starbucks is an outstanding book that tells a compelling story about a company, its history, and meaning. *Clicks and Mortar* by David Pottruck, former CEO of Charles Schwab, and Terry Pierce is another excellent example in this genre. Steve Jobs's speeches to Apple employees inspired them to think differently.

One fine example of a written articulation of a group's inspiring identity comes from the U.S. Navy. Here are excerpts from the USS *Montpelier* Command Philosophy, written by the commander of the USS *Montpelier,* a Los Angeles-class nuclear attack submarine commissioned in 1993 that has won several of the navy's highest awards for its stellar performance:

Montpelier Command Philosophy

Montpelier is a warship, designed to steam into harm's way and win. Our flesh and blood bring this ship to life. We are stewards of one of the most capable warships in the history of mankind. These thoughts provide a framework for executing that stewardship and for building the teamwork that will enable us to fight and win in war.

Honesty. Honesty provides the foundation of trust that is essential to teamwork. I expect and require that you be completely honest in your communication with your shipmates. I will do the same with you. At times, this will be painful, but it is extremely important that we have the facts when making decisions and that our relationships are based on mutual trust. I pledge not to kill the messenger.

Integrity. Do the right thing; don't take the expedient path. If you are not sure what the right thing is, and you have the opportunity, ask. If you can't, trust your judgment and training. This requires a great deal of courage, but if you act honestly and faithfully in this regard, you will not be second-guessed.

Teamwork. No ship, department, or division is successful as a one-man show. Teamwork is the key to success. Our actions must reinforce this concept. If you find yourself thinking about a problem in the command and the word "they" pops into your head, think again. "We" will solve problems together. I am not one of them and neither are you.

Open-Door Policy. Leadership is about setting priorities. If you have an idea for a better way, suggest it. My door is always open to discuss your concerns. I trust that you will use the chain of command when possible.

Caring Leadership. Know your people. Translate your caring into tangible results. Get them off the ship when you can. Ensure they are ready for advancement. Make a difference in their lives.

Mistakes. Honest mistakes come with the territory. I will make some and so will you. The keys to success are establishing enough backups so that we don't make a critical mistake and recognizing and learning from the mistakes that we do make. Your tour will be filled with many ups and downs. It is not how many times you fall that will determine your success. Your honesty, integrity, and determination to fight on, will.

Fitness and Sleep. Submarining requires stamina. Fitness, nutrition, and sleep are key to your decision-making. As General Patton said, "Fatigue makes cowards of us all." Take care of your body and your mind. I do not judge you on how long you work or how long you stay awake, but on how effective you are.

Standards. The standard is excellence in all we do. Aristotle said, "We are what we repeatedly do. Excellence, then, is a habit." Our reputation is determined in a large part due to how we execute routine evolutions, our personal appearance and the appearance of our ship. It is the sum of each of our actions. Set the standard.

Fun. Submarining is an extremely challenging and demanding profession. At times the hours will be long and the work hard, but it is important that we have fun while fulfilling our responsibilities.

Work/Life Balance and Community. Success at work is interwoven with success at home. I consider it vital that we balance our military duties with our roles in the family. Take advantage of opportunities to make time for your family and work hard to keep your professional role and your family role in perspective. It is also important that our families understand the importance of our mission and that we recognize the sacrifices that our family members must make in order to fulfill our duties. Service is a team effort. I will make an effort to create a family environment on board and to support our families. A successful command has a family atmosphere, where every member takes pride in being a part of the team.

Personal Development. I expect every Sailor to be working towards his personal and professional development, and I will support your actions in these areas.

Critical Self-Assessment. Our ability to improve is dependent on our ability to analyze the causes of our failures and to take action to address those problems. At times, we will formally critique events. The intent is to fix the problem, not the blame. Honesty is critical to this process.

Decision Making. I will not establish a lot of detailed policies to spell out and legislate decisions on board. I will balance the long- and short-term needs of each individual, the ship, and the U.S. Navy. If time allows, I will make every effort to explain my decision, but there will be times when it is not practical and I expect you to trust my judgment.

Equality. We swear to support the Constitution of the United States, which states that all men are created equal. I expect you to treat each of your shipmates, our families, and our visitors with dignity and respect.

Ambassadors. Overseas, we are ambassadors of the United States. At home, we are representatives of the submarine force, the Navy, and the U.S. Military. Our behavior and actions should reflect the pride and responsibility we feel as members of an elite military organization.

Service and Reward. My ultimate goal is that you consider your service on board one of the most rewarding experiences in your life. This requires that you resolve to better yourself, your ship, your shipmates, and your country. Each night when you go to sleep ask yourself, "What have I done today to make myself a better man? How have I made *Montpelier* a better ship? Have I been a faithful steward of one of our country's most valuable assets, this ship and the outstanding Sailors who fight her?"

These are my thoughts, just words on paper. Our actions together make them a reality and the key to our success.

The *Montpelier* Command Philosophy provides us with a sense of the leader who wrote it, someone who was direct, honest, and personally committed to the mission. It is a sincere, authentic expression of this leader's beliefs. It addresses the fundamental issues of inspiring identity.

Effective leaders know that they must provide meaning so that others will commit to and make sacrifices for the sake of the mission. To provide meaning, leaders must make an investment of their time to fully understand it and to communicate it in way that reaches the hearts and minds of the people they lead. The Command Philosophy reflects a great deal of thought and preparation, and it has the mark of a leader willing to make sacrifices for the sake of the mission and for the sake of the people he leads.

Creating and communicating an inspiring identity to help people become mission-minded make a difference in their performance. Great leaders know the importance of connecting people through a shared identity that inspires them. Leaders who shirk this responsibility, often because they let the urgent tasks crowd out the significant ones, fail to fully engage and fire up the people they lead.

Review, Reflection, and Application

- ❑ A successful organization must have a clearly defined identity that inspires people. A few ways to inspire people include appealing to their personal identity and the aspects it shares with the organization's identity, establishing the value of your work to clients and/or society, providing a challenge, or bringing something new to the world.

- [ ] Try to find multiple ways to communicate your organization's inspiring identity, including stories, visual depictions, facts and figures, pithy sayings, and video clips. Doing this will help you reach people with different thinking and learning styles. The written word is especially effective because people can come back to it.

- [ ] Share! Share! Share! Keep the inspiring identity in front of people.

- [ ] So what? To increase connection among people at work, individuals need to see that their organization's identity adds something to their personal identity. Can you articulate your company's identity in a clear, compelling, and understandable fashion? Are there aspects of your company's identity that fit with how you like to think about yourself?

CHAPTER 9

Delete What Devalues

The next cultural element in a connection culture is *value,* which I will refer to as *human value* as we take a deeper look at this element. Human value recognizes that all people have feelings and that being valued matters to them. It also recognizes that appreciating a person's talents and helping him achieve his potential encourages him. He becomes fired up and feels more connected to the group when he is part of a culture that embraces human value.

The American Revolution and America's subsequent economic success are vivid historical examples of the power of human value. King George III's inability to understand human value forever connected his legacy to a monumental managerial blunder: losing the American colonies.

From Outpost to Empire

What motivated a ragtag collection of colonial citizen-soldiers who were woefully ill-equipped and ill-trained to defeat the most powerful military in the world? One reason was King George III's condescension toward the colonists. At the time of the Revolution, many Englishmen regarded the colonists as inferior. With that prevailing view the king felt he could throw his considerable weight around and get away with abusing his power. To raise money to pay the debts incurred by England while defending the colonies during the French and Indian War, King George levied taxes on the colonists without their consent. Given the chip on the colonists' shoulders resulting from the disdainful attitude of the English, that was the straw that broke the camel's back. The colonists viewed taxation without representation as a violation of their rights as citizens of the British Empire and equated it to being treated as slaves by the English king and Parliament.[1] The king's actions provoked the fury of a people who already felt scorned. Thanks to King George, the thirteen separate colonies came together, formed a militia and, with assistance from France and financial resources from Holland, won their independence.

The brand-new country expanded human value with a series of actions. With the adoption of the Constitution and the Bill of Rights, America protected the voting and civil rights of white males. The nation's increasing investment in education and public infrastructure empowered its citizens, giving them greater opportunities to achieve their potential and realize what would become known as the American Dream.

The economic opportunity and social mobility increased engagement and the sense of connection among Americans. They responded by producing extraordinary economic growth. Historian Gordon Wood wrote in his Pulitzer Prize-winning book, *The Radicalism of the American Revolution,* that in less than fifty years America went:

> [from] less than two million monarchical subjects . . . on the margin of civilization . . . [to] a giant, almost continent-wide republic of nearly ten million egalitarian-minded bustling citizens who not only had thrust themselves into the vanguard of history but had fundamentally altered their society and their social relationships . . . [Americans] had become, almost overnight, the most [free], the most democratic, the most commercially minded, and the most modern people in the world.[2]

Today, America is the undisputed global economic leader. In addition to America's economy being the largest in the world, it is a fertile culture for innovation. Of the recent Nobel laureates in economics, three-fourths reside and work in America. American movies account for more than 80 percent of global box-office revenues. American pharmaceutical companies invent more drugs than all other drug companies outside the USA combined. America accounts for 40 percent of the world's technology expenditures, and American venture capital firms are far more numerous than firms outside the USA.[3] As it turned out, expanding human value in America was not only right, it was also wise! Human value contributed to a modern-day miracle: the transformation of an outpost of civilization into the most powerful national economy the world has ever witnessed.

Human value in a culture is, first of all, about treating people with respect and dignity, and second, about empowering them to achieve their potential. In the rest of this chapter, I'll describe how leaders can remove obstacles in an environment that make people feel devalued, and in the following chapter, I'll recommend how leaders can add elements to an environment that make people feel valued.

First, Do No Harm

In the age-old Hippocratic Oath that physicians take before they begin to practice medicine, they pledge first to do no harm to their patients. Likewise, the first step for any leader who wants to engage his or her people and increase connection is to eliminate behaviors and attitudes in the culture that do harm to people by devaluing them. Let's consider a few areas where you can do this.

1. *Eliminate disrespectful, condescending, and rude behavior.* People are devalued when they are subjected to uncivil behavior in the workplace. Obviously, physical aggression is wrong. Less obvious is verbal abuse, especially if it is not clear that the instigator intended to harm the target. Remember the childhood phrase "sticks and stones may break my bones, but words will never hurt me"? The truth is, words can and do hurt.

Most of us have witnessed managers berating the views of lower-ranking employees during meetings. These senior managers may reject others' ideas without explaining their reasons why. Likewise, they may assert that their views are obviously superior without allowing a dialogue on the pros and cons of their position or on the alternatives. This approach is just one example of incivility in an organizational culture.

Uncivil behavior can take many forms, including interrupting someone who is speaking, giving someone the silent treatment, or completely ignoring someone. Generally, any action meant to humiliate, intimidate, undermine, or destroy a colleague in the workplace is uncivil and should be forbidden.

Unfortunately, patronizing behavior at work is too common. A 2001 survey of 1,180 workers found that 71 percent of them reported experiencing disrespectful, rude, or condescending behavior from superiors or coworkers within the last five years. One out of every four of these workers confronted the offender, and 75 percent of them experienced retaliation because they spoke out.[4]

Disrespectful, condescending, and rude behavior must be eliminated from the corporate culture if we are to engage and energize people. When someone consistently exhibits uncivil behavior, he needs to know that it damages connection and is unacceptable. It should be made clear that continuing such behavior will bring about the perpetrator's removal. A leader who allows someone in his chain of command to commit uncivil behavior also needs to be held accountable.

If left unchecked, uncivil behavior in the workplace will spread. Second-in-command leaders tend to adopt the leadership practices of their bosses—whether they are civil or uncivil. The only way to eliminate this corrosive behavior is for leaders to model civil behavior and take action to remove people who have proven themselves incapable of reform.

2. *Go easy on the criticism.* Another devaluing behavior is excessive criticism. Wise leaders know how to provide useful input with the goal of improving performance without adding undue pressure that could contribute to a loss of confidence.

Joe Torre, the phenomenally successful manager of the New York Yankees, knows to go easy on his players. His approach stems from personal experience with the frustration that came during disappointing times in his career as a ballplayer. "I hit .360 one season, and I hit .240 another year, and I felt I played equally hard both years," said Torre in a *Fortune* magazine article that heralded him as a model for today's corporate managers. Former Yankees superstar Paul O'Neill said this about Torre: "Joe doesn't put added pressure on you or act differently toward you because you're not hitting well or playing well. Players pick up on these things." Yankees pitcher Mike Stanton added, "With Joe you really don't have to look over your shoulder, because you'll lose confidence in yourself long before Joe loses confidence in you. He'll say, 'I remember what you did for me. I remember what you did for this organization.'"[5]

A good leader can take care of those he leads and still be performance-oriented. Task excellence is critical to his success. Leaders don't reach the top of their professions by avoiding performance problems. The difference is that they place themselves in the shoes of their employees to understand how to get things done in a way that shows appreciation and respect. They improve tasks by nurturing a healthy work culture that values people and helps them feel more connected to their team.

3. *Minimize unnecessary rules and excessive controls.* Unnecessary rules and excessive controls devalue people by making them feel that they are not trusted or respected. A leader who overcontrols his people will not engage or energize them. Micromanaged employees are more likely to feel disconnected. Another universal human need is to have a reasonable degree of autonomy or freedom to do our work so that we might have a greater sense of control and experience personal growth as we develop new skills and expertise.

Napoleon was known for micromanaging. After the French Revolution and the Reign of Terror that succeeded it, Napoleon restored order to the nation. Unfortunately, he didn't know when to limit his controlling tendencies. According to historian James MacGregor Burns, Napoleon was not a bloodthirsty tyrant but a control fanatic. He controlled the press, books, theater, workers' associations, and public demonstrations.[6]

To teach the youth of France to respect the country's laws, for example, he took control of French schools from the locals and hired instructors who were required to teach from the same syllabus and textbooks. The result of this overcontrolling approach was that children fled to Catholic schools. And when Napoleon enacted conscription for military duty, the lives of soldiers became so draconian and restrictive that as word spread, it produced "mass resistance of a sustained, endemic character," according to historian Isser Woloch.[7] Draft evaders were so desperate, they mutilated themselves or escaped over the Pyrenees mountain range to avoid military duty. The French did not want to be micromanaged.

French citizens wanted freedom, not an overbearing ruler to dictate every aspect of their lives. After the deaths of several hundred thousand French soldiers from the catastrophic campaign in Russia during 1814 and Napoleon's later military defeat at Waterloo in 1815, his popular support waned. The self-appointed emperor learned that many of his supporters were of the fair-weather variety. In the end the British exiled Napoleon to the island of St. Helena.

In the business world, the destructiveness of an excessively controlling person was demonstrated in the fall of the Pullman Palace Car Company in the late 1800s. George Pullman, an entrepreneur and engineer, created a successful company that built luxury railcars. As business boomed, Pullman built a company-owned town for his employees and named it after himself. He believed that a clean, orderly environment without saloons or other illicit attractions would produce superior workers. Pullman, Illinois, had a population of eight thousand people living in 1,400 housing units owned by Pullman and rented to the employees. It contained a school, a park, a library, a church, and other necessities of modern life. The company maintained the streets and lawns. Rent was deducted from employees' paychecks. To ensure that his rules were followed, Pullman hired "spotters" who identified troublemakers. If any of Pullman's rules were violated, an employee could be evicted on ten days' notice according to the terms of the rental agreement. Pullman kept his finger on the pulse of every aspect of his workers' lives.

Although Pullman thought the workers should be grateful that he was allowing them to live in a Pullman-built utopia, they didn't see it that way. Many complained about the lack of freedom and often left to visit Chicago's neighborhoods nearby. In 1893 when the nation experienced a depression, Pullman was forced to lay off a fifth of his workforce and reduce wages by 25 percent for the remaining employees. Despite this downturn, workers who lived in Pullman's town continued to pay rent at current rates. The financial squeeze unleashed an underlying torrent of discontent among workers. The combination of employee disengagement and reduced pay triggered a backlash. In May 1894, Pullman's workers went on strike, and across the country other railroad workers, who were members of the labor union, joined the strike. After mass violence erupted and $80 million in property was damaged, President Grover Cleveland sent federal troops to protect the mail delivered via railroad, and the courts ordered an end to the strike.[8] Eventually, Pullman's company went bankrupt. Like Napoleon, Pullman learned the true feelings of the people he led, feelings that were hidden in good times.

George Pullman's leadership is an extreme example of a well-intentioned leader who didn't understand the people he led. Leaders can learn from Pullman's unfortunate experience that controls—rules, processes, and procedures—should be maintained only if experience has proven that they are necessary and they produce benefits for the organization. Clearly, some controls are necessary and beneficial to ensure efficiency and concentration of effort, but excessive control is a sure way to contribute to employee burnout. Leaders need to strike the right balance between giving people freedom and maintaining a minimum of controls and rules.

4. *Eliminate excessive signs of hierarchy.* Leaders who display excessive signs of their power and position, like proud peacocks showing off their feathers, devalue others. In a sense, their pride is in competition with everyone else's pride. When a leader tries to hog all the trappings of success, he crowds out recognition for others. Wise leaders err on the side of understatement.

Consider Stan Gault, who led the Rubbermaid Corporation to become one of the most respected corporations in America. Shortly after he retired from Rubbermaid, the board of directors of the Goodyear Tire and Rubber Company asked him to take over the CEO's job. Goodyear's performance had suffered, and the company had taken on a heavy debt load to repurchase stock from corporate raider Sir James Goldsmith. Gault had to act fast. An early move was to send several messages to employees that he was on their side. He linked his pay to the performance of Goodyear stock, and he declared to all that he was willing to place his faith in the people of Goodyear and that together they would restore the company to its former glory.

Gault inherited his predecessor's office on Goodyear's famed Mahogany Row. The office was large and required a considerable amount of lighting. He immediately unscrewed most of the light bulbs to cut costs. The word quickly spread at Goodyear. It wasn't long before everyone knew that when Gault asked employees to reduce expenses, he would be sacrificing too.[9]

Other leaders have taken similar actions. When A. G. Lafley became the CEO of Procter & Gamble and began its remarkable turnaround, he reduced the excessive executive office space and used the reclaimed space for an employee resource center. When Charles Schwab had to lay off workers in 2001, he declined to take any salary that year, provided generous severance packages to laid-off workers, personally established a $10 million trust to fund laid-off workers' education expenses and, in a historical first, granted them stock options. At Intel Corporation, the former chairman and CEO Andrew Grove sat in an open cubicle and parked in the general parking lot like all other employees.

Each of these leaders eschewed excessive signs of hierarchy and showed by their actions that they were willing to share in the sacrifice with everyone else. In one interview Carolyn Dewing-Hommes and I conducted, a person shared her disgust over a chief financial officer who communicated the need to reduce travel expenses and yet went against company policy and flew first class on short trips. Such leaders who are insensitive to others reduce connection because they create an emotional distance between themselves and most workers. When workers feel that leaders are enjoying all the fruits of the company's success or are not feeling any pain when times are difficult, they resent it and feel that selfish leaders are taking advantage of them. Conversely, leaders who make sacrifices for the good of the team elevate their employees and acknowledge their value.

5. *Get rid of devaluing leaders.* Jack Welch, the former head of General Electric, talks about how much he values the right leadership style and how he believes it affected trust and cooperation across GE. In GE's 2000 Annual Report Welch had this to say:

> We have to remove . . . the "go-to" manager, the hammer, who doesn't share the values, but delivers the numbers . . . on the backs of people, often "kissing-up and kicking down" during

> the process. We have to remove these managers because they have the power in themselves to destroy the open, informal, trust-based culture we need to win today and tomorrow.
>
> We made our great leap forward when we began removing [these types of] managers and making it clear to the entire company why they were asked to leave—not for the usual "personal reasons" or to "pursue other opportunities," but for not sharing our values. Until leaders develop the courage to do this, people will never have the full confidence that these soft values are truly real. There are undoubtedly a few [of these managers] remaining, and they must leave the company, because their behavior weakens the trust that 600,000 people have in their leadership.

Over time GE has done just that. The company identified leaders who didn't value people, even if they were making their numbers, and fired them after they had proven that they were unable or unwilling to change. The devaluing leaders described by Jack Welch damage the connection with people they are responsible for and therefore don't deserve to lead them.

6. *Replace devaluing severance procedures.* If it becomes necessary to reduce compensation expenses by eliminating positions, do it in a way that allows people to preserve their dignity. The consulting firm McKinsey & Company helps former employees find new jobs and stay connected to the firm's alumni network. Other companies take a far different approach. They pack up a person's belongings, shut off his e-mail access, and have him escorted to the door. Absent an indication of potential for violence, this approach is damaging to the employee-employer relationship. People will take note of how their former colleagues were treated.

By implementing the suggestions noted here, you will reduce the elements in an environment that make people feel devalued. In the next chapter, we'll look at actions you can take to fire up people by making them feel valued.

Review, Reflection, and Application

- ❑ Human value exists in an organization when everyone understands the basic psychological needs of people, appreciates their positive, unique contributions, and helps them achieve their potential.

- ❑ Human value is about treating people with respect and dignity and empowering them to achieve their potential. America's break with England and its subsequent rise as an economic power demonstrate how human value can have a profound effect on people.

- ❑ Several types of behavior and attitudes in an organization should be removed because they devalue people. The following actions will increase human value.

    1. Eliminate disrespectful, condescending, and rude behavior.
    2. Go easy on the criticism.
    3. Minimize unnecessary rules and excessive controls.
    4. Eliminate excessive signs of hierarchy.
    5. Get rid of devaluing leaders.
    6. Replace devaluing severance procedures.

- ❑ Do you recall examples of devaluing behavior that you have experienced or witnessed at work?

- [ ] So what? The element of human value can make or break your success as a leader. When people are devalued, they lose their motivation to excel at work, and they may want to retaliate against those who devalue them. By eliminating devaluing behavior, organizations can increase trust and cooperation among employees. What have you done lately to ensure that everyone you are responsible for leading is consistently treated with the respect and recognition that bring out the best in them and that you hope for yourself?

CHAPTER 10

Dial Up the Value

The flip side of eliminating behaviors and attitudes that devalue people is adding elements that enhance people's value. These positive measures effectively empower people to achieve their potential.

David Neeleman, the CEO of jetBlue airlines, is an excellent example of a leader who adds elements to the workplace environment that increase employees' sense of being valued. He refers to his colleagues at jetBlue as fellow "crew members" rather than employees. He meets with 95 percent of new crew members on their first day of work. Neeleman makes it a point to know the names and stories of many people in the jetBlue organization. Each week when he sets aside a day to fly the airlines' routes, he connects with the crew while working alongside them. His actions speak volumes to the crew about how much he values them.

Here are a few ways you can do this:

1. *Make a human connection with as many people as possible.* Leaders need to acknowledge individuals. There's no easier way to

show you value people than to learn about them and use their names when you speak with them. Knowing names and personal stories helps leaders make a powerful emotional connection with people in a short time. Leaders from the top down should be expected to know the stories of the people with whom they frequently come in contact. If you lead a large number of people, you can make human connections by meeting them, maintaining eye contact, saying something to them as you pass in the hallway, and acknowledging what they say to you. When leaders model this behavior, others will follow suit. Although it sounds so obvious, many leaders don't do this.

Connection is increased by helping employees know each other's stories too, especially those of people who frequently interact with each other. One way to learn more about others is to maintain an intranet-based directory that includes employees' names, pictures, and any information they feel comfortable sharing such as interests outside of work, favorite books, movies, quotations, and other information that communicates their unique stories. Giving individuals an opportunity to express themselves brings the color of human personality into the workplace.

2. *Treat and speak to employees as partners.* Treating people below you in your organization's hierarchy as equals rather than as inferiors enhances their sense of personal value. Remember, leaders make eye contact, say hello, and use the person's name, if possible, when you walk by an employee. Aloof behavior only communicates that someone is not worth acknowledging. Treat employees as partners too. Don't expect them to do personal errands for you. Think of others as partners who play different roles from yours. You will keep them connected and energized as they sense the respect you show them.

3. *Help employees find the right roles.* Another way to show appreciation is to help people better understand their abilities, temperaments, and values. Each individual is a unique combination of natural and learned cognitive capabilities. Assessment tools enable people to identify their skills, temperaments, learning styles, thinking styles, and values. Providing these resources to people will help leaders place them in the roles where they will be most likely to excel. People who excel will be more likely to receive genuine recognition and respect, and well-deserved praise is encouraging and strengthens connection.

Although many companies provide personality testing to selected leaders, few offer it to people throughout the organization. Chances are it has been a tool to help those leaders build a well-balanced team of people based on their personality types. This is a good start. But more tools should be used if you are serious about bringing out the best in the people you lead.

Being in a position that fits an employee's strengths so that he performs well is essential to give him a sense of value. I refer to this as the *right role.* When a person is in the right role, he knows it and so do his peers because he is good at what he does.

Several factors determine whether someone is in the right role. One factor is that the job fits well with the individual's personality and abilities.

A second factor is that it presents the right degree of challenge. If our jobs are too easy, we will grow bored. If too difficult, we will become overly stressed. When we are in the right roles, however, we become immersed in our work to such an extent that we become unconsciously absorbed and lose a sense of ourselves and of the passing time.

Psychologist Mihaly Csikszentmihalyi has conducted extensive research on the subject with participants from around the world. When the participants' work provided the right degree of challenge, they consistently described the feeling of being so caught up in their work that they lost a sense of self and of time, a state that Csikszentmihalyi called "flow."[1] His research shows that being in the right role, a role that creates flow, helps meet the universal human need for personal growth. In effect, when we are performing a challenging task that gives us a sense of flow, we are personally growing. Csikszentmihalyi believes that a person who is in a state of flow actually feels the sensation that comes when the brain is making new neural connections. Whatever the case, the flow that occurs when we are personally growing brings out the best in us. It fires us up.

A third factor that contributes to being in the right role is that the job is consistent with the way the individual thinks of herself, her identity, and her values. The industry, the particular company, and the specific job all say something about her identity. When her job is consistent with her identity, she will be more engaged; when it's inconsistent with her identity, the job will contribute to her disengagement. When her identity is inconsistent with the identity of the company—for example, a vegetarian working at a steakhouse—she is in the wrong place and is unlikely to be excited about her work.

4. *Educate, inform, and listen to employees.* Educating, informing, and listening to employees enhances their sense of value. If you don't let people know what you are thinking, if you don't inform them and hear their points of view, they'll probably assume the worst. When people can't see the direction they are headed, they naturally experience anxiety. Conversely, when you inform and listen to them, they will be grateful that you recognized them and valued their ideas and opinions. With informa-

tion and understanding comes a greater sense of security and optimism that the future is bright. We will explore this issue in greater detail in the chapters ahead.

5. *Decentralize decision making.* Allowing people to make decisions shows them that you respect their abilities and judgment and that you value them. Many firms over the last hundred years decentralized decision making. Decentralization gained momentum when Peter Drucker persuaded Alfred P. Sloan Jr. to decentralize decision making at General Motors Corporation. It also grew when manufacturers worldwide began to adopt the Lean Manufacturing practices of Japanese companies, replacing the overspecialized, assembly-line mentality with teams that developed broader knowledge and skills and had greater autonomy. One contributor to the continued success of Toyota Motor Company and its Lexus Luxury Division is the higher-quality and lower-cost benefits resulting from the Toyota Production System. This management approach combines a high degree of team-based training, autonomy, decentralized decision making, and responsibility for continuous improvement.[2]

Companies have learned from experience that decentralized decision making improves morale by giving more control to lower-level employees. It also improves effectiveness when decisions are made by the people who are closest to the relevant information. Having more decision-making authority lets people feel more in control, more respected, and more appreciated. Greater autonomy, so long as it does not exceed a worker's level of competence, fires up people. It leads to a greater sense of connection and engagement.

6. *Recognize the human need for work/life balance.* Finally, we all have times when things outside work require our undivided

attention. It may be the health of a loved one or our own health. Leaders need to balance giving employees time off for urgent needs in their personal lives with being fair to other employees who have to do more work when a colleague is away.

Encouraging people to get sufficient rest and relaxation outside work is an important part of keeping people from burning out. Toward the end of most days, President Franklin Delano Roosevelt held a gathering for cocktails and poker where the only rule was that no one could talk politics. He cherished the time to relax and recharge. It revived his energy level and helped him maintain the optimism to lead America out of the Depression and through World War II. It also stimulated his creativity. During a vacation that some members of the press criticized FDR for taking, the president conceived the Lend Lease program to provide military assets to Great Britain in its hour of need.[3]

People in the creative professions, including writers, musicians, and thought leaders, have long recognized the value of rest and relaxation to stimulate their creativity. Many of them retreat to quiet and relaxing settings to free themselves from the distractions of day-to-day life and release their creative energies. Prayer and meditation are frequently cited as practices that stimulate creativity.

Successful leaders, from America's founders to Joe Torre, imbued the culture they were responsible for leading with human value. Leaders such as Napoleon and George Pullman failed, at least in part, because they didn't understand what motivates and demotivates people. Wise leaders know that applying human value in the work culture can make a world of difference by connecting and firing up people, ultimately affecting their own success or failure as leaders.

Review, Reflection, and Application

- ❑ Six ways to increase human value in an organization are as follows:
  1. Make a human connection with as many people as possible.
  2. Treat and speak to employees as partners.
  3. Help employees find the right role.
  4. Educate, inform, and listen to employees.
  5. Decentralize decision making.
  6. Recognize the human need for work/life balance.

- ❑ How does your organization fare in the six ways to increase human value?

- ❑ So what? It's not enough to get rid of aspects in an organization that devalue people. To achieve maximum connection, you must also increase human value in ways that show people you want to help them reach their potential at work.

CHAPTER 11

THREE BENEFITS OF KNOWLEDGE FLOW

In June of 2000 the combative Durk Jager resigned as CEO of Procter & Gamble after a tenure that had lasted only seventeen months, the shortest in the firm's 165-year history. When he left P&G, its stock had declined 50 percent, it had lost $320 million in the most recent quarter, half of its brands were losing market share, and the firm was struggling with morale problems.

Jager was replaced by a low-key, quiet, and thoughtful P&G veteran named A. G. Lafley. Although Jager had questioned the competence of many P&G employees, Lafley immediately assured them that he knew they were capable of restoring the marketing powerhouse to its former greatness. Lafley's long career in marketing had taught him how to glean insights by listening to P&G's customers. Now he sought to do the same by listening to P&G's employees. Lafley turned to Jim Stengel, heir apparent to the chief marketing officer, and asked him to conduct a survey to find out what employees thought should be done.

Although senior managers were considering several new business initiatives at that time, P&G's employees felt something different was needed. They wanted a renewed commitment to marketing, more time to listen to customers, the results of programs to determine rewards rather than the quantity of programs launched, and more disciplined market planning.

After P&G implemented employee suggestions, the number of employees who strongly agreed with the statement "We're on the right track to deliver business results" soared from 18 percent to 49 percent in just twelve months. And in a little more than two years after taking over from Jager, Lafley restored P&G to profitability, and the organization experienced a 70 percent increase in its stock price. *Fortune* magazine heralded Lafley as the "un-CEO" for his emphasis on listening and "hearing [P&G employees] out practically one at a time."[1]

Lafley turned P&G around in part because he increased the cultural element I described earlier as *voice.* The expanded term for this element is *knowledge flow.* There are three primary benefits to stimulating knowledge flow: it increases connection and fires up people, it helps leaders make better decisions, and it increases innovation.

Benefit #1:
Knowledge Flow Increases Connection and Fires Up People

Knowledge flow communicates to people with less power in an organization that they are appreciated and respected enough to be informed and heard, and that their ideas can make a difference. As we discussed about human value, the affirmation and inclusion energizes and engages people. Knowledge flow says that no one has a monopoly on good ideas; an idea or way of thinking originating at the bottom of the organization's hierarchy just may be the one that helps the organization achieve its mission. The story of A. G. Lafley's turnaround of P&G illustrates that knowledge flow can help restore the confidence, optimism, and energy of employees.

History provides many examples of leaders who reduced knowledge flow to their detriment by marginalizing or eliminating individuals who held different viewpoints. In every case the people became disconnected, disengaged, and eventually turned on their leaders.

The French Jacobin revolutionary leader, Maximilien Robespierre, is known primarily for instigating the Reign of Terror in 1793. During that time anyone perceived to be against the French Revolution was sent to the guillotine. When Robespierre took control of the Jacobins, the leftist revolutionary group that overthrew King Louis XVI, he aggressively eliminated anyone who disagreed with his radical views. Robespierre's suspicions of others contributed to his increasing isolation. Ultimately, his former supporters turned on him and sent him to the guillotine in 1794.[2]

Julius Caesar contributed to his demise by curtailing knowledge flow. Near the end of his life, Caesar treated the Roman Senate with disrespect, and he became dictatorial. He acted as if the Senate was a mere advisory council. He became intolerant of views that differed from his own. In 44 BC a group of republicans led by Cassius and Brutus murdered Caesar after his behavior led them to believe that he would abolish the Senate and make himself king of the Roman Empire.

Leaders' careers have advanced or receded over knowledge flow. One reason that Dwight D. Eisenhower was made Supreme Allied Commander of Europe during World War II was that he encouraged knowledge flow by seeking, listening to, and considering the opinions of others.[3] Several legendary military leaders were passed up for the position because they had reputations for not listening to others. Generals MacArthur and Patton wouldn't listen to the British, and British General Montgomery wouldn't listen to the Americans.

Eisenhower, however, was open-minded and confident without being arrogant or condescending. He displayed these character traits as he considered one of the most important decisions in his lifetime: when to launch the D-Day assault and send two hundred thousand soldiers into harm's way. General Eisenhower brought together all fourteen of his direct reports, not to take a vote but to hear and weigh their points of view. Only afterward did he make the decision to go.

The attention Eisenhower paid his direct reports helped to make them more dedicated to him and their common mission. After he decided to launch the attack, he went out to circulate among the soldiers and encourage them before they departed. Eisenhower was on the airfield with the Eighty-second Airborne in the evening, assuring them that the massive force assembled for the assault would make them victorious. This action increased knowledge flow. The time with the troops communicated he valued them too. As word passed among the men that General Eisenhower was there in person, the troops had a psychological boost going into one of the most difficult military missions they would ever face.

Benefit #2:
Knowledge Flow Helps Decision Makers Make Better Decisions

Knowledge flow helps organizations improve performance by leveraging the experience, insight, and information among people throughout the entire organization. Leaders who don't inform and listen to people throughout the organization, especially those who hold different points of view, are effectively isolating themselves from potentially valuable knowledge that will contribute to better decision making.

The story of Andrew Grove and Intel illustrates how knowledge flow in a culture improves decision making. In his book

Swimming Across, Grove, the former chairman and CEO of the microchip powerhouse, recounts his experiences of growing up in Hungary during the Nazi occupation and under Communist control following World War II and then immigrating to America. From these personal experiences Grove developed an appreciation for an open-minded culture and its benefits, having lived in fascist and totalitarian environments in which the ruling regime controlled speech, education, and the arts.

As a new student in an American classroom, Grove encountered a telling contrast to life in Hungary. He was shocked that American students questioned their instructors. Hungarian students were expected to listen to and regurgitate their teachers' views. One did not dare challenge the powers that be, at least not openly.[4]

Years later, when Grove rose to head Intel, he promoted an open-minded culture within the company by encouraging what he called "constructive confrontation"—people shared opposing views in a way that their differences would not become personal. He recognized that people needed to discuss alternative ideas and viewpoints without letting emotionalism creep in and thereby break down future communication. Grove also praised what he called "helpful Cassandras," the people usually on the front lines of the business who, because of their strategic sense and proximity to the marketplace, were early to identify strategic inflection points that would impact their business. (Cassandra was the priestess of Greek mythology who used her powers of prophecy to predict the fall of Troy.)

In his book *Only the Paranoid Survive,* Grove recounted how constructive confrontation and helpful Cassandras played a role in helping him make a major decision in his career: to have Intel exit the DRAM semiconductor business and focus on microprocessors. At that time the prevailing view among people at Intel and in the semiconductor industry was that the discounted prices offered by Japanese competitors were attributable to dumping excess inventory. They believed that Japanese firms could not possibly be making a profit at the prices they were selling DRAMs in the US market.

A handful of helpful Cassandras at Intel, however, believed otherwise. In their view, the Japanese firms were actually making money at the lower prices because their superior quality allowed them to scrap fewer defective chips. If that was true, Intel was in for trouble ahead because its quality was far below that of its Japanese competitors. As the internal debate at Intel progressed and Grove heard from the helpful Cassandras, he eventually realized that they were right. Grove made the decision to exit one of Intel's largest businesses before it got ugly.

His decision turned out to be prescient. The Japanese took over the global DRAM market and competitors with higher cost structures suffered while Intel focused on the lower-volume but higher-margin microprocessor business. Within a little more than a decade following Grove's decision, Intel grew from one of many competitors in the overall semiconductor market to the largest nonproprietary manufacturer of semiconductors in the world, with revenues larger than its next three competitors combined. So successful were Grove and Intel that *Time* magazine named him Man of the Year in 1993.[5] By encouraging constructive confrontation at Intel, Andrew Grove increased knowledge flow in the Intel culture and improved decision making.

Like Andrew Grove, wise leaders as far back as ancient times warned of the dangers of self-delusion and learned that there is wisdom in seeking advice. The Greek orator Demosthenes cautioned in the fourth century, "Nothing is easier than self-deceit. For what each man wishes, that he also believes to be true." King

Solomon, one of the most revered kings of Israel who was known for his wisdom, wrote more than thirty admonitions in the book of Proverbs advising that it is wise to be humble, to seek the advice and knowledge of others, and to listen to them. Solomon observed that pride leads to failure and that humility is necessary for wisdom (Prov. 16:18, 11:2). Leaders should not rely solely on their own judgment; Solomon stated that the foolish seem confident in their ways, but the wise seek and consider the advice of others (Prov. 12:15). More recently, the Scottish philosopher and historian David Hume declared, "When men are most sure and arrogant they are commonly most mistaken."[6]

Several of America's founding fathers were especially well-known for seeking the advice of others. George Washington was a good listener who sought the opinions of others; he rarely spoke during most meetings. Like his fellow Virginian, Thomas Jefferson listened attentively but seldom spoke. Benjamin Franklin was renowned worldwide for his wisdom, breadth of knowledge, sense of humor, and tendency to listen more than to speak. During the twilight of his life, as the Constitutional Convention was concluding in Philadelphia, he addressed his fellow delegates, and in support of the newly drafted document he said:

> For having lived long, I have experienced many instances of being obliged, by better information or fuller consideration, to change opinions even on important subjects which I once thought right but have found to be otherwise. It is therefore that the older I grow the more apt I am to doubt my own judgment and to pay more respect to the judgment of others.[7]

Ben Franklin's lifelong experience had taught him that it was wise to maintain a healthy skepticism about his own views and to carefully consider the views of others. Earlier in life, he had written an editorial defending free speech and a free press; he noted that it was wise to let everyone publicly express views and, in doing so, more likely that the best ideas and courses of action would emerge from public debate.

During World War II British Prime Minister Winston Churchill demonstrated his belief that knowledge flow was critical. Churchill was so concerned about getting accurate information to enable him to make decisions about the war that he established a group outside his generals' command, the Statistical Office, to provide an independent viewpoint and confirm important facts. Churchill, an avid student of history, knew the risk to leaders who didn't receive accurate assessments, and he feared that his presence and personality might keep his generals from telling him bad news.[8]

According to historian Doris Kearns Goodwin, FDR wanted to hear many points of view before making decisions, so he deliberately appointed people with diverse views to his cabinet. He also looked for people who were not afraid to challenge him or each other. The disagreements among his cabinet members often became a matter of public knowledge. For Roosevelt, it was a small price to pay, provided it made him a better decision maker.[9]

When a leader becomes isolated by surrounding himself with yes-men or by being closed to other viewpoints, he sets himself up for failure. The list is long of leaders who maintained false preconceptions until it was too late to change direction. The Catholic Church of the Middle Ages refused to acknowledge that the sun, rather than the earth, was the center of the universe despite Galileo's proof. This and other challenges to Catholic doctrines contributed to a decline in its influence and the rise of Protestantism and humanism in Europe. (Perhaps this was one experience that persuaded the Catholic Church to allow at least some internal debate. In 1760, the church began formally appointing a person to the role of *advocatus diaboli,* the "devil's advocate," who would argue against the case for the canonization of an individual being considered for sainthood.)

In the year 1520, Montezuma, the last Aztec ruler of Mexico, mistook the Spanish conquistador Cortés to be the Aztec god Quetzalcoatl. Cortés demanded that Montezuma hand over his empire, and he did without putting up any resistance and despite clear signs that Cortés was not a deity (the Spaniards demanded gold and worshiped Jesus and the Virgin Mary). Cortés had fewer than six hundred men, seventeen horses, and ten artillery pieces at his command compared to Montezuma's thousands, yet Montezuma was easily tricked. Montezuma's failure to fully consider the situation cost him the Aztec Empire and his life when his own people stoned him.[10]

Holding on to false preconceptions continues to have negative consequences. Senior management at Lucent didn't listen to scientists who warned of the need to develop a new optical technology, OC-192, and then watched as Nortel introduced it to great success in the 1990s. As a result of this and other instances of management failure, Lucent nearly had to file bankruptcy.[11]

Before the 1986 launch of the *Challenger* space shuttle, some engineers at NASA knew that the O-rings on previous shuttle flights had shown evidence of damage, yet they rationalized away the problem. Their doubts didn't surface until *Challenger* exploded. Boston College sociologist Diane Vaughan, in her book *The Challenger Launch Decision,* describes NASA's culture in which engineers who were aware of the potential problem were reluctant to bring the issue out into the open. Pressure to meet the launch schedule and a culture that exalted a "can do" attitude and looked down on those who called attention to potential obstacles that were less than obvious made engineers reluctant to share their concerns, absent clear-cut evidence of a problem. Unfortunately, not all problems present themselves in obvious ways.[12]

Seven years after the *Challenger*'s loss, some of the same issues resurfaced when the *Columbia* space shuttle exploded. Once again NASA's senior managers were unaware of NASA engineers' concerns about damage to the shuttle that occurred upon its launch. NASA engineers had gone so far as to analyze the potential for damage and had even involved people at the Boeing Corporation without alerting senior management. Rather than aggressively addressing potential problems as they arose, once again NASA's culture encouraged engineers to move cautiously below the radar screen of senior management. In essence, the engineers feared to speak candidly to those in power in part because leaders failed to actively seek out the engineers' concerns.[13]

Investigations into the terrorist attacks on September 11, 2001, indicated that the lack of knowledge flow contributed to America's intelligence failure. Poor communication between the FBI and the CIA and between the FBI field offices and its headquarters meant that analysts lacked access to information that might have helped them spot a pattern of activity suggesting a potential plot.[14] This is another chapter in a long history of American intelligence failures that should have identified impending attacks. America failed to see the inevitability of its involvement in World War I until many citizens were killed when a German U-boat sank the British luxury liner *Lusitania*. Likewise in World War II, America failed to understand the emerging threat of the Axis powers until Pearl Harbor was attacked and more than two thousand Americans lost their lives.

We're slow to see changes in the way the world works, even

when the evidence is in front of us. When we refuse to hear and consider other people's opinions, we isolate ourselves from change, and we don't stand a chance of maintaining a realistic view. Mark Twain expressed the sentiment well when he said, "It's not what you don't know that hurts you. It's what you know that ain't so." The bottom line is that when we fail to seek and consider the views of others, we commit self-sabotage.

Cognitive scientists have begun to understand why it is so difficult for us to recognize when our views are no longer true. Their research has revealed that our brains are slow to replace existing beliefs with new ones because it requires more energy and effort, more brain power if you will, to process new ideas. It's simply easier to allow our brains to work on autopilot and accept our existing beliefs, even if they are untrue. Only a constant flow of information that challenges our preconceptions will cause us to question our existing beliefs and consider alternative views.[15]

History teaches us that knowledge is power. It is power precisely for its usefulness in helping leaders and decision makers choose optimal courses of action. Knowledge flow in a culture is the only proven antidote to our human susceptibility to maintain false preconceptions. Leaders who promote knowledge flow are deemed wise for their successful decisions and their winning organizations.

Benefit #3: Knowledge Flow Increases Creativity and Innovation

The third benefit of knowledge flow is an increase in creativity and innovation. When knowledge flows vertically up and down the chain of command and horizontally across an organization, it empowers people and makes them more effective. Encouraging the creative energies of people at all levels can lead to remarkable results, as the following story from World War II illustrates.

After the Americans landed on the beaches of Normandy on D-Day and secured their initial positions, they began to push deeper into France. In June 1944, about ten miles inland, they approached the Normandy countryside that the French call the Bocage. This area consisted of plots of land that farmers separated with hedgerows rather than fences. The hedgerows were made of several feet of packed soil topped off with brush and vines. When a Sherman tank attempted to go over the top of the hedgerows, the nose of the tank popped up, exposing its thin underbelly to Nazi antitank fire. Allied military planners had spent so much time concentrating on the D-Day landings that they hadn't fully considered the problems in hedgerow country. The Sherman tanks' vulnerability caught everyone by surprise.

At first, the Americans tried blasting the hedgerows open so the Sherman tanks could then breach the holes created by the explosions. Unfortunately, the explosions gave the Nazis advance warning of where the tanks were going. Nearly a month after D-Day, the Allies were falling behind schedule primarily because of the problems created by the hedgerows and the adeptness of the Nazis' hedgerow defense.

One day, in a discussion between officers and enlisted men, the idea arose of mounting saw teeth on the front of the tank. Many of those present laughed at the suggestion. One soldier, however, took the idea seriously. Sergeant Curtis G. Cullen, a cab driver from Chicago, immediately designed and built a hedgerow-cutting device made from steel rails that the Nazis had used to defend the beaches. When tested, Cullen's device, backed by the Chrysler engines powering the Sherman tanks, sliced right through the hedgerows.[16]

Sherman tanks mounted with Cullen's device looked like rhinoceroses, so the soldiers began calling them *Rhinos*. Within days of the idea's origination, it was on the desk of General Omar Bradley, head of the First Army. He attended a demonstration of the Rhino and immediately ordered five hundred of Cullen's devices. In two weeks, 60 percent of the First Army's Sherman tanks became Rhinos. In General Bradley's account of the war, *A Soldier's Story*, he credited the Rhinos for getting the First Army through the hedgerow country in time to crush the Nazi army in France.[17]

Commenting on the speed with which the hedgerow-cutting device moved from idea to implementation, historian Stephen Ambrose observed:

> That didn't happen in other armies . . . I'm convinced that this came out of being a participating member in a free society . . . Rommel did not have a suggestion box outside his door. Eisenhower did. Bradley did . . . Hitler thought totalitarianism is by far the most efficient form of government . . . but as Eisenhower wrote to his brother on September 1, 1939, the day the war began: "Hitler should beware of the fury of an aroused democracy." Well, the U.S. Army of World War II became the tip of the spear of that aroused democracy. And we just did wonderfully well.[18]

The US Army benefited when Sergeant Cullen's hedgerow-cutting device idea quickly made its way to General Omar Bradley, who was open-minded enough to consider and act upon it. Ultimately, knowledge flow contributed to the Allies' liberation of France.

In the business world, innovation often comes from the people closest to clients and competitors. At Starbucks a store manager in

West Los Angeles was experimenting with beverages and a blender she had brought to the store. Her curiosity led to the creation of the Frappuccino, a frozen drink that became a multi-hundred-million-dollar business for Starbucks stores and a major new business for a Starbucks and PepsiCo joint venture to bottle the Frappuccino and sell it through grocery stores.[19]

The danger to nations that reduce knowledge flow is apparent throughout history. By isolating themselves and their countries, the leaders of civilizations have missed opportunities for innovation and growth. China in 1400 had the best and largest fleet of ships in the world (over a period of three years the Chinese built or refitted 1,681 ships). With their enormous fleet, the Chinese sailed to Indonesia, Arabia, East Africa, and India. Gradually, however, the Chinese emperor's attitude toward the benefits of foreign travel shifted as he favored domestic agriculture over maritime interests. By 1436, the Chinese were diverting resources from maintaining the ships, and by 1500, anyone who built a ship with more than two masts was subject to the death penalty. In 1525, the Chinese authorities ordered all oceangoing ships to be destroyed and their owners arrested.[20]

A period of Chinese isolation from the rest of the world began. At the time of the ships' destruction, China led the world in innovation. It had developed gunpowder, deep drilling, printing, paper, porcelain, cast iron, and the compass. China's isolation, however, prevented it from knowing about developments beyond its borders, the ideas and information that had contributed to its high rate of innovation when Chinese ships were sailing the world. In recent decades, economic reforms and social freedoms have reconnected China to the broader world, resulting in increased Chinese economic growth.

Like the Chinese civilization, the Arab-Islamic civilization became isolated in the sixteenth century as its leaders adopted the view that the world beyond them had little to offer. As a result of the isolationism adopted by the Chinese and Arab-Islamic civilizations, both began a period of steady decline in innovation and economic output. Meanwhile, European innovation and output increased with expanding conquests in the New World and the opening up of European society following the Enlightenment. The lack of knowledge flow in the Chinese and Arab-Islamic civilizations contributed to their fall from being global leaders in innovation and creativity, just as Europe's increased knowledge flow contributed to its rise.

Knowledge flow fires up people by giving them a voice and meeting the human psychological needs for respect, recognition, and belonging. By helping leaders make better decisions and increasing innovation, the last two benefits of knowledge flow contribute to improving an organization's performance and, by doing so, further fire up people. Research has shown that people who work for better-performing organizations are more engaged in their work.[21] In Chapter 12, we'll examine specific actions you can take to increase knowledge flow in your work environment.

Review, Reflection, and Application

- ☐ Knowledge flow exists when everyone in an organization seeks the ideas of others, shares ideas and opinions honestly, and safeguards relational connections.

- ☐ Knowledge flow in an organization communicates that people are appreciated and respected, helping to increase connection and engagement.

THREE BENEFITS OF KNOWLEDGE FLOW

- ☐ Knowledge flow helps leaders be their most effective by leveraging the experience, insight, and information among people throughout the organization.

- ☐ Leaders who fail to seek and consider the opinions of others eventually will succumb to the negative consequences generated by false preconceptions.

- ☐ Andrew Grove of Intel made one of the best decisions in his career by encouraging knowledge flow and learning from it. George Washington, FDR, Winston Churchill, and other significant leaders also benefited from a leadership style that increased knowledge flow.

- ☐ The US Army benefited from knowledge flow when Sergeant Curtis Cullen's idea for the Rhino tank quickly made its way to General Omar Bradley in time to help the Allies liberate France during World War II.

- ☐ Cultures that isolate themselves from external knowledge flow shut off a flow of ideas that increase innovation.

- ☐ Knowledge flow in your organization should be sufficiently robust up and down the chain of command, across departments and business units, and from outside the organization so that everyone benefits from an extensive marketplace of ideas and know-how.

- ☐ So what? Knowledge flow is critical to firing up people, helping leaders learn so that they can make better decisions, and stimulating innovation. Where do you see that knowledge flow is high and where it is low in your organization? Are some parts of your organization isolated from knowledge that might benefit them? Are you and others in your organization intentional about increasing knowledge flow?

CHAPTER 12

Increase Flow

After seeing that leaders who increase knowledge flow benefit from it and that leaders who don't risk failure, you might ask what you can do to ensure that knowledge flow is maximized in your organization. The following are several steps I recommend to increase knowledge flow in your culture.

1. *Hold ongoing knowledge-flow sessions.* Leaders stimulate knowledge flow by regularly holding sessions with employees in which they share information about important issues facing the organization and near-term action plans they are considering. The leader encourages employees to share what they believe is right, what's wrong, and what's missing from his or her thinking. The frequency, length, and size of these sessions can be tailored to particular segments of employees. Sessions are conducted at all levels of the organization.

Unlike the typical staged town hall meeting in many organizations, the knowledge flow session is characterized by honest dialogue. Key to its success is an environment in which participants feel safe to share their ideas and opinions.

Results from knowledge flow sessions are shared with all participants, and valuable ideas arising from the sessions are executed. Employees feel more connected and become more fired up as they are informed, they are heard, and they see their ideas implemented. Because few leaders do this well, it is wise for most leaders to get outside assistance to design and implement the knowledge-flow session process as well as see it modeled.

BENEFITS OF KNOWLEDGE FLOW

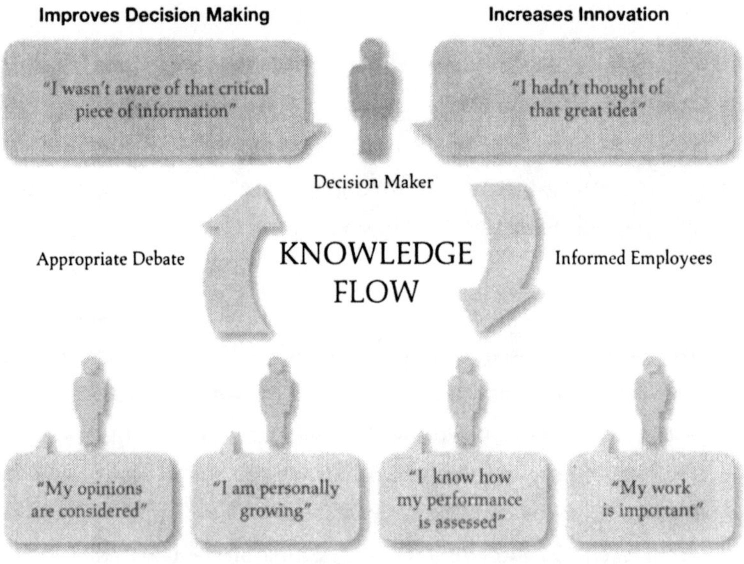

2. *Use your intranet to make information easily accessible.* Too many leaders are reluctant to make information available to all employees. The benefit of making information widely available will far outweigh the risk of information leaking to external sources. Leaders

will gain from having more knowledgeable, fired up employees who feel that leaders respect, value, and trust them enough to make important information available to them. The Charles Schwab Corporation makes an extensive number of strategy and competitive-analysis reports available to all employees on the firm's intranet platform dubbed the "Schweb." The Schweb is a repository of information ranging from commonly used forms and contact information to topical reports and business segment updates.[1]

McKinsey & Company is another firm that makes an abundant amount of information available to employees. The firm maintains a database of previous reports generated by its consultants. Potentially sensitive contents about clients have been removed before the reports are posted to the database. McKinsey also maintains a database of experts throughout the firm that can be sorted by area of expertise and by office.[2] This practice leverages the vast unwritten knowledge and experience of McKinsey's people.

3. *Promote a culture of responsiveness.* McKinsey & Company has an informal rule that everyone should return telephone calls within twenty-four hours. It enables a person who needs knowledge to identify someone who might hold it, contact him, and have a response within twenty-four hours.[3] This practice is a powerful way to leverage knowledge that might otherwise go unused for the benefit of the firm.

4. *Ask people to be inquisitive.* Better-informed employees are more likely to identify critical pieces of information to solve business problems and spot opportunities. I like the term Peter Drucker once gave to the contributions of educated employees who shared an opposing point of view. He called it "informed

dissent."[4] Leaders should ask employees to seek to understand their business, client attitudes, and competitors' actions so that they can bring informed dissent to the organization's decision-making process. General Electric does this by thinking of and describing itself as a "learning company." Among other things, GE encourages employees to recognize best practices outside the company and in other business units across GE, all for the purpose of continually strengthening their businesses.

5. *Encourage external awareness.* When Andrew Grove of Intel made the bold decision to exit the DRAM memory business and focus on microprocessors, much of the information that aided his decision came from external sources noted by Intel employees. They compiled quality data on Japanese-versus American-made memories, Japanese manufacturing practices, and other industry-related operations because they wanted to understand their competitive position and how it might change in the future.

Leaders will benefit by encouraging employees to consider what external knowledge might be valuable and to seek it out. This practice will help protect the company from what Harvard Business School professor Clayton Christensen has called "disruptive technologies" (new offerings that change your industry's paradigm).[5] It will also help your company discern opportunities to be the instigator of disruptive innovation.

6. *Increase the diversity of participants.* People with diverse knowledge, experiences, abilities, thinking styles, and temperaments see things differently. Leaders can improve the creativity in a group's problem identification and solution seeking by including people with diverse backgrounds. When holding knowledge flow sessions with groups of employees, be sure to include a mix of people

from different departments and professional backgrounds, and make them aware that you are counting on them to offer fresh perspectives.

7. *Seek other views and reward those with the courage to speak up.* Leaders must encourage employees to express their points of view, especially when they see things in a different light from leaders or the majority of their colleagues. Typically, individuals who hold views not aligned with those held by leaders or by the majority of their colleagues are punished and thought of as troublemakers.[6] Socrates, Sir Thomas More, William Wallace, Martin Luther King Jr., Mahatma Gandhi, Alexander Solzhenitsyn, Nelson Mandela, and many, many other courageous heroes openly expressed their views and were imprisoned or killed for doing so.

Machiavelli wrote in the sixteenth century that nothing is more dangerous than trying to bring about change. According to research on group conformity, individuals within a group consider dissenters to be less competent than people who hold the majority view. That's why we fear to speak out and do so only in an environment where trust and honesty are highly valued. For these reasons, great leaders must not only tolerate the expression of all differing viewpoints but also encourage it. Leaders would be wise to follow the example of Andrew Grove, who celebrated people for spotting strategic inflection points on the horizon. Openly admitting that "no one has a monopoly on good ideas" and asking people to share what they believe is "right, wrong, or missing" from your thinking is a badge of wisdom and courage, not a sign of weakness.

8. *Promote a culture of experimentation.* From the many ideas generated in a diverse and open culture with high knowledge flow, it is not always clear which single idea or course of action is superior.

Great leaders have embraced experimentation as the way to find ideas that turn out to be the most effective in practice. Experience is the best teacher. By creating pilot projects to test new ideas, leaders benefit from the additional knowledge brought by experience.

The wisdom of experimentation reminds me of the story of Thomas Edison performing an extraordinary number of experiments as he sought to develop the light bulb. It is said that as his assistants grew frustrated with mounting failures, Edison calmed them by sharing this perspective: "Yes, it's true that we have worked long and hard and haven't found what we're looking for. But the results of our work have been excellent. We have a list of fifty thousand things we know won't work."[7] We don't expect leaders to experience Edison's high rate of failure before achieving success. However, to an extent that's the attitude a leader must take: we as an organization learn with each completed experiment, and we must strive to take into account the insights from our failed experiments so that we may improve our batting average on future decisions and courses of action.

9. *Safeguard relational connections.* It is important in all communications to be sensitive to the feelings of other people. Politely asking someone to do something is preferable to giving orders. Using a respectful tone is better than talking down to someone. Insensitive communication styles impede knowledge flow because people will naturally react in a defensive manner. Individuals who regularly show insensitivity should be made aware of it and coached to change their behavior. People who are insensitive in communicating with others may be unaware of it. Although they may not like hearing it, once they see proof of the reactions on the part of their colleagues, they will begin to appreciate the need to change.

Observing the Chain of Command

Critics might label this knowledge-flow approach of informing people and broadly gathering and considering input as another form of management by committee. It is not. I am not advocating that a leader delegate decision making to a committee or group. I believe in seeking the best ideas and then making decisions that must be followed by all, even the informed dissenters. This system combines a diversity of ideas with unity of action.

Even after people have expressed their views and the decision has been made, there will be times when people do not agree. The duty of dissenters is to respect authority and abide by it to the best of their ability. A decision-making hierarchy, or *chain of command* as some call it, is a system that has been proven to work extremely well. A decision-making hierarchy defines who is responsible for decisions and holds that person accountable for the decisions he makes. It is responsive and efficient because it doesn't require the time and effort to achieve consensus from all parties when time is of the essence. Furthermore, a decision-making hierarchy concentrates resources by requiring everybody to act on the decision that has been made.[8]

The antithesis of a decision-making hierarchy is direct (or pure) democracy in which everyone gets a vote on most decisions. Direct democracy is rare because it takes time to inform everyone and hear views. It is also problematic because majority viewpoints are not always well-informed, especially on complex issues. Few people have the time to delve deeply into every issue so that they are prepared to make knowledgeable decisions. Direct democracies have at times produced disastrous results. The direct democracy in Athens executed one of history's greatest teachers, Socrates, for not believing in the Athenian gods. America's Founding Fathers rejected direct democracy in favor of a republic, or representative democracy, that places decision making in the hands of elected leaders.

One leader who wisely decided against the majority view in the late 1970s was Donald Regan. Then head of Merrill Lynch, he decided to launch the first cash management account. Most people in Merrill Lynch at the time feared the new product would cheapen the firm's image and eventually hurt business results. The product development staff, however, favored it. Regan considered the views of both sides and decided to go forward. As it turned out, the cash management account attracted billions of dollars and millions of new clients to Merrill Lynch. The product became one of the most popular innovations in financial services history. It brought many American households into the capital markets for the first time and provided attractive funding for economic expansion during the final decades of the twentieth century.[9]

I believe the optimum solution is a decision-making hierarchy that includes broad participation and input from others, especially on the most important decisions facing the organization. This preserves the benefits of a chain of command by clearly assigning responsibility and accountability for making decisions while bringing the broad experience, ideas, and opinions of others to the decision makers' attention. This practice gives participants a greater sense of ownership in decisions, and it enhances connection.

Review, Reflection, and Application

❑ Nine ways to increase and stimulate knowledge flow are as follows:

1. Hold ongoing knowledge-flow sessions.
2. Use your intranet to make information easily accessible.
3. Promote a culture of responsiveness.
4. Ask people to be inquisitive.
5. Encourage external awareness.
6. Increase the diversity of participants.
7. Seek other views and reward those with the courage to speak up.
8. Promote a culture of experimentation.
9. Safeguard relational connections.

- ☐ Would your colleagues say you actively seek the views of others and seriously consider them? Do your colleagues seek the views of others and seriously consider them?

- ☐ So what? When a high degree of knowledge flow exists in your organization, you can be sure that people are more engaged, decision makers will make better decisions, and innovation will be greater, all of which contribute to organizational success.

PART III

The Fire Starts With You:

Become a Person of Character and Connection to Ignite the Team Around You

In Part III you will learn . . .

- why connection would never occur if it weren't for the right kind of people whose actions increase connection.
- there are three types of people who affect connection: intentional disconnectors, unintentional disconnectors, and intentional connectors.
- none of us is perfect and we all need to be intentional about developing the character strengths that increase connection.
- others can help us become aware of the blind spots in our character that decrease connection.
- we improve our character and connection with others by maintaining high-trust relationships, undergoing periodic relational checkups, and knowing the stories of great people who exhibited character strengths.

CHAPTER 13

People Who Connect

In the Introduction of this book I described how my personal experiences, and in particular my wife's bouts with cancer, influenced my thinking about connection and organizational culture. Other events in my life, as well as my study of culture and leadership, have shaped my views about the cultures I want to be a part of, the type of leaders I want to follow, and the person and leader I aspire to become.

How about you? What experiences in your life have shaped your beliefs about work culture and leadership? How about your experiences growing up, including the way your parents, siblings, teachers, and coaches treated you? Did some of them inspire you and others discourage you? How did your friends and peers affect you? Did some of them bring out the best in you and others bring out the worst? How have the mentors or leaders you've had influenced you?

I sincerely hope that reflecting on these questions will provide you with insights to guide your journey in life to places and relationships that will bring out the very best in you personally and professionally.

Oxygen for the Soul

After spending years thinking about and studying the issues of culture, leadership, and connection, I'm convinced that they are critical to my personal success and well-being as well as the success of any group of people that I am a part of. My family, neighborhood, church, children's schools, business, town, state, nation, and the world are affected in positive and negative ways by culture, leadership, and connection among people.

Unfortunately, because these issues are less tangible, it's easy to take them for granted. Tasks and processes are out there in the open for us to see and quantitatively measure. Connection, like oxygen, tends to be less obvious. The clearest way we know that connection is missing is to experience environments where it is in abundant supply and environments where it isn't. Only then do we feel and appreciate the difference.

Unlike oxygen deprivation, the effects of connection deprivation take place gradually so that our decline in performance and well-being can be slow and steady. And therein lies the danger. Absent an awareness of connection and an appreciation for its positive effect on our lives, we could be gradually disconnecting ourselves and not be aware of it until the damage is done.

The high degree of connection that my family and I experienced with family, friends, and health-care professionals during the course of Katie's treatment for cancer woke me up to the connection deficiency in my life. After experiencing that degree of connection, I cannot return to the imbalanced life I was living before. Sure, there will be times and seasons when I need to focus more on tasks and less on relationships, but they shouldn't be extended times that drain the life out of me. By asking yourself the questions in Appendix A, you too can begin to consider the state of connection in the cultures you live in.

Which Type Are You?

Each of us acts in ways that increase connection at times and decrease it at others. In general, though, individuals tend to fall into one of three categories when it comes to connection. We are intentional disconnectors, unintentional disconnectors, or intentional connectors.

Intentional disconnectors are people who infect others with beliefs and behaviors that cause disconnection. They mock the idea that inspiring identity, human value, and knowledge flow are desirable in and of themselves. They're selfish and will intentionally manipulate people to get their way. Emotionally, they live alone because they fear being vulnerable and genuine with others. They may put on a front, a smiling mask, but on the inside they are gradually becoming empty and depressed souls. Some intentional disconnectors have serious psychological problems, and mental health professionals would categorize them as neurotic. Others embrace values that are disconnecting, such as doing whatever is necessary to get ahead, despite what is commonly accepted as right. Believe me, I know from personal experience that working with an intentional disconnector is a nightmare. That's why we need to be aware of them and to stay out of their destructive paths.

Based on press accounts, it would appear that "Chainsaw Al" Dunlap, the former CEO of Sunbeam, was an intentional disconnector. He relished intimidating people and ruling like a dictator. As the inevitable consequences of his leadership style played out,

Sunbeam's performance woes intensified until Dunlap was dismissed.

Unintentional disconnectors represent the majority of people. Although they believe inspiring identity, human value, and knowledge flow are desirable, they lack sufficient self-knowledge to see that their behavior reduces connection. They suffer from blind spots, destructive habits that increase disconnection. They may order others about as if they were children. Or perhaps they are unable to consider constructive criticism without turning their wrath on the messenger. Or maybe they are unable to connect with the people they lead and are unaware of it. Whatever the case, unintentional disconnectors decrease connection without realizing it. For the most part, we drift toward becoming unintentional disconnectors, and we must exert intentional effort to realize it and change.

Take me, for example. Early in my career, my supervisor told me that some people whom I was responsible for leading didn't feel I gave them adequate feedback about their performance. More specifically, they sensed I wasn't telling them when they did something that I disliked. Through this feedback, I realized that by communicating only positive, encouraging aspects of the employees' performance, I was not doing what was best for them. In addition, I needed to be honest with employees when they did something I disagreed with so that they might learn from the situation and adjust their behavior. Because people sensed I wasn't being completely candid with them, the connection between us was lessened. Now that I am aware of this blind spot, I'm careful to tell people when I have qualms about their actions.

My story isn't unique. Many leaders become aware of their blind spots and their behaviors that foster disconnection when they receive constructive feedback from a supervisor or executive coach. With coaching and ongoing processes put in place to measure their progress, many grow to become better leaders.

When we make a commitment to change and open ourselves to honest feedback about the effects of our behavior, we begin the journey to become people who reach our potential and help others reach theirs. I can't emphasize enough that we naturally drift toward becoming unintentional disconnectors, and the only way to consistently increase connection is to become intentional about developing into the type of person who increases it.

Over the course of my life, I have been fortunate to learn from people who consistently enhance connection. Some have been leaders in the traditional sense while others have not. I have personally met some while I have learned about others by studying their lives, reading their letters and speeches, and reviewing what others have written about them. I've recounted a few of their stories in this book. Still others you would not know because they are not in the public eye.

Intentional connectors are full of life, a sense of purpose, and genuine joy compared to most people you meet. Inevitably, they are wise about themselves and about life. They increase connection in the cultures of which they are a part because they embody inspiring identity, human value, and knowledge flow. They combine a steadfast dedication to reaching performance excellence and accomplishing their mission while nurturing a culture that creates connection.

Although there is much to admire in intentional connectors, that doesn't mean they are perfect. No one is. And that leads me to a major point that we'll discuss in the following chapter.

Review, Reflection, and Application

- [ ] Which of the three types of people who affect connection are you: an intentional disconnector, unintentional disconnector, or intentional connector?

- [ ] Most of us are unintentional disconnectors and are unaware that our actions are inconsistent with our values.

- [ ] Take a moment and identify one or more intentional connectors in your life. What is it about them that you would like to emulate?

- [ ] So what? We all naturally drift toward becoming unintentional disconnectors. We must exert intentional effort to develop the habits that increase connection.

CHAPTER 14

The Journey to Connection

Becoming an intentional connector requires a personal journey. No one is perfect. Even great leaders who have made significant contributions stumble at times. FDR, one of my personal heroes, failed to get behind federal anti-lynching legislation, interned innocent Japanese-Americans during World War II, and had an affair that left his wife, Eleanor, emotionally scarred for life. In 1939, FDR, bowing to anti-Semitism in the USA, refused to allow entry of the SS *St. Louis,* and nearly all of its 937 Jewish passengers died in concentration camps when the ship, unable to find a safe haven, returned to Europe. Even though FDR was responsible for these actions, we can still admire him for his courage and optimism in facing polio and guiding America through the Depression and World War II.

The Battle Within

Each of us faces an internal conflict between doing what is right and what is wrong. In the Bible, the apostle Paul wrote that he wanted to do what was right though often another part of him yearned to do otherwise. Sigmund Freud wrote of the ongoing conflict inside us between our desires and our conscience. Responding to the query in the *Times* (London): "What is wrong with the world?" British author G. K. Chesterton simply replied: "Dear Sir, I am."[1]

We all can relate to an inner battle. On the one hand, we want to eat that dessert, but on the other hand, we don't. We want to tell the person questioning our viewpoint that he's nuts, yet we know better because we might learn something from him, or we might damage our relationship. We don't want to take the time to get to know some of the people we work with, yet we know we should.

In the movie *Crash,* which won best picture at the 2005 Academy Awards, we see people over the course of a thirty-six-hour period at their worst and at their best. In one scene, Police Officer Ryan, played by actor Matt Dillon, abuses his power while allegedly frisking a woman for concealed weapons. Later in a separate incident, he courageously risks his life to pull the same woman out of a car moments before it explodes. Although Officer Ryan's acts are extreme, like him, we also commit some acts that are right and others that are wrong. It's just a matter of degree. Put in situations where constraints on our behavior don't exist, we might commit acts that we find difficult to imagine today.

If we are honest with ourselves, we know that we are capable of right and wrong, even good and evil. The personality that is hard-wired in us at birth, the habits we develop over a lifetime, and the culture we live in influence our behavior and whether we act in a way that is right or wrong. For example, people are more likely to share information with one another if they have trusting temperaments, they habitually share information with others, and they work in cultures where others routinely share information.

This is why character development is so important. Character helps us to do the right thing even when internal and external pressures make us want to do otherwise. Martin Luther King Jr., Nelson Mandela, Harriet Beecher Stowe, William Wilberforce, Winston Churchill, and Mahatma Gandhi are just a few notable leaders who stood against evil despite tremendous pressure to maintain the status quo. Their character strengths of courage, compassion, and justice gave them a clear understanding of what was wrong and the determination to do what was right.

It's no different in an organization. People who are most likely to increase inspiring identity, human value, and knowledge flow in a dog-eat-dog culture do so because they have character strengths that guide them to do what is right. Character strengths provide us a moral compass to know what is right and the desire to do what is right. Without character strengths to guide us, we are more susceptible to going with the flow of our temperaments, our habits, and our current culture.

Character and Connection

To see how certain character strengths relate to the elements in a connection culture, consider some leaders highlighted in earlier chapters and how their character strengths led to actions that improved connection.

Purpose, optimism, and vitality increase inspiring identity. Steve Jobs's desire to find a meaningful purpose for Apple Computer and his hard work to achieve it reflect these character strengths. The same could be said for Richard Feynman's desire to tell engineers the reason for their work on the Manhattan Project.

Kindness and a love of people increase human value. David Neeleman at jetBlue airlines models these character strengths when he takes time to meet with 95 percent of jetBlue's new crew members. Howard Schultz at Starbucks shows his concern by making health-care insurance and stock options available to most of Starbucks's employees, many of whom work part time.

Humility, open-mindedness, and curiosity increase knowledge flow. A. G. Lafley's continuous seeking of opinions and ideas from the people at Procter & Gamble is a reflection of these character strengths. George Washington also had these character strengths: he was known as a listener who considered others' views.

When the beliefs and behaviors of people in an organization live up to the standards of good character I just mentioned, it creates the inspiring identity, human value, knowledge flow, and ultimately, the connection necessary to become a great organization.

The Character Connection Thrive Chain diagram shows clusters of character strengths that specifically link to the elements in a connection culture.

THE CHARACTER CONNECTION THRIVE CHAIN

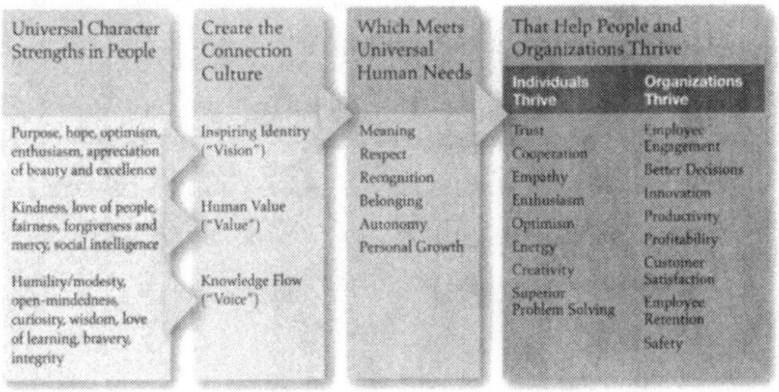

Research is beginning to confirm that organizations that advance character strengths experience superior performance. According to a 2004 Aspen Institute and Booz Allen Hamilton study of corporate behavior, companies that attained superior financial results were far more likely to have written value statements promoting ethical behavior/integrity, commitment to employees, honesty and openness, and a drive to succeed (what might also be called vitality or work ethic).[2]

Once we accept that character strengths are desirable, we must ask ourselves how to develop them in ourselves and in the people we are responsible for. There are several ways to develop character strengths that will help individuals become intentional connectors and improve connection in organizations. Let's take a look at each of them in the next chapter.

Review, Reflection, and Application

- ❑ Each of us faces an internal struggle between doing what is right and what is wrong.

- ❑ By developing character strengths, we are better able to recognize what is right and have a greater desire to do what is right.

- ❑ A person who has good character will increase connection. The Character Connection Thrive Chain illustrates how specific clusters of character strengths act to increase the elements that, in turn, increase connection.

- ❑ So what? To increase connection among a group of people requires that group members have the character strengths—or beliefs and behaviors—that increase connection. In fact, it's essential if we hope to meet our potential and that of our organizations.

CHAPTER 15

Developing Character Strengths and Connection

Many people today recognize the importance of becoming more intentional about developing character. A 1999 survey conducted by Public Agenda, a nonprofit, bipartisan group, found that American adults ranked "not learning values" as the most significant problem facing young people today.[1] More schools adopted character-building programs after President Bill Clinton in 1996 called for an increase in character education, and President George W. Bush tripled the federal budget for such activities.[2]

Understanding and embracing character strengths provide a mental map to guide our behavior. A mental map is a belief pattern that resides in one's mind. Our minds are filled with a variety of mental maps, such as one about what is required to be healthy, one about how automobiles work, and one about how the solar system is structured. A mental map about character strengths gives us a standard that we will aspire to achieve.

In recent years, neuroscientists discovered scientific evidence supporting the existence of mental maps. At the moment when we have an insight that constructs a mental map, scientists have observed the occurrence of high-frequency gamma waves and an increase in adrenaline that gives us a feeling of pleasure and boosts our energy level. They believe that these measurable occurrences are evidence that the brain is forming a neural connection to record and help us remember our newly acquired belief.[3]

In addition to the evidence that supports the formation of mental maps in our brains, there is compelling evidence that a level of awareness of character strengths exists in our brains at birth. This has traditionally been referred to as our "conscience." The evidence comes from the work of a group of leading psychologist-scholars who have identified twenty-four character strengths that have been universally recognized by moral philosophers and religious thinkers throughout history. These character strengths include creativity, curiosity, open-mindedness, love of learning, perspective, bravery, persistence, integrity, vitality, love, kindness, social intelligence, citizenship, fairness, leadership, forgiveness and mercy, humility/modesty, prudence, self-regulation, appreciation of beauty and excellence, gratitude, hope, humor, and spirituality.[4]

The character strengths are seen across tribes and nations and across centuries. They are found in Buddhism, Christianity, Confucianism, Hinduism, Islam, Judaism, and Taoism. Data from more than thirty nations support their existence. When University of Illinois professor Ed Diener studied isolated tribes such as the Masai in Africa and the Inuit in Greenland, he concluded they readily recognized the twenty-four character strengths.[5]

This group of psychologist-scholars believes that the practice of these character strengths improves mental and physical health, and they have begun a movement—called positive psychology—to encourage people to embrace and practice them. Led by Martin Seligman, the former president of the American Psychology Association and a professor of psychology at the

University of Pennsylvania, their early work that identifies the character strengths was published in 2004 by the American Psychology Association in *Character Strengths and Virtues: A Handbook and Classification.*

Character strengths should be encouraged in organizations too. Employees who exhibit selfless sacrifices for the sake of the team, honesty, a strong work ethic, and other character strengths that benefit the organization should be celebrated and rewarded.

How to Develop the Character Strengths of Intentional Connectors

The question of how to develop character strengths has been considered since antiquity. The following practices improve character and increase connection:

1. *Develop habits that reflect character strengths.* To become intentional connectors, individuals need to develop the habits that reflect character strengths. Many intentional connectors exhibit intentionality and discipline to develop character strengths. Coach John Wooden's Pyramid of Success was comprised of traditional character strengths. So were the Rules of Civility that influenced George Washington. In *The Autobiography of Benjamin Franklin,* the statesman and inventor described the character strengths he aspired to have and his efforts to improve upon one virtue each week.[6] He wrote that good behavior was difficult to achieve, given our inclination to do otherwise. The only remedy was to concentrate on character development and, through repetition, build the habits of doing what is right.

Abraham Lincoln developed an understanding of character from reading the Bible, Shakespeare, biographies of people he admired (including Washington and Franklin), and the ancient classics. Lincoln's strong sense of justice gave him the backbone as a twenty-three-year old army private to protect an innocent Native American who wandered into a camp that Lincoln commanded during the Blackhawk War. Lincoln stood between the innocent man and the soldiers who wanted to kill him until they backed down. Lincoln's strong moral compass gave him the backbone to emancipate slaves and resist the Confederate secession during the Civil War. In *Lincoln's Virtues,* author and historian William Lee Miller explains that Lincoln's intentionality in building character gave him the "moral confidence" to do what was right despite the overwhelming pressure he faced at times not to.[7]

2. *Build high-trust relationships with people who want to develop good character.* We need to build in checks and balances to protect us from self-deception, the blind spots that I referred to earlier. The recognition that we all have blind spots led French political philosopher Charles-Louis de Secondat, Baron de Montesquieu, to advocate checks and balances in the governance of nations. Montesquieu's 1748 masterpiece, *The Spirit of the Laws,* influenced America's founders to adopt a political system with checks and balances.[8]

Good advisors who care enough to give us honest feedback are one means to help us see our blind spots. During her more than four-decade reign, Queen Elizabeth I had in Sir William Cecil a first-rate counselor. Cecil was not only hardworking and steadfastly dedicated to the queen; he was also humane and wise. Although Queen Elizabeth had other advisors, she trusted none more than Cecil. Even after Cecil's years of hard work began to take their toll on him, the queen continued to rely on his judgment to help her think through matters.[9] Unlike Queen Elizabeth, Frederick the Great (who will be discussed later on) was utterly alone. He trusted no one. Perhaps this lack of connection and his emotional isolation played a role in Frederick's mental and physical decline.[10] Steve Reinemund, chairman of PepsiCo Corporation, is a more recent example of a leader who has stated publicly that he has a group of close friends with whom he meets regularly, and they encourage and challenge him in his responsibilities as a spouse, father, and leader.[11]

Spending time with friends who are intentional connectors gives me the encouragement I need to develop good character. Because each one of us strives to improve his character, we help one another. We meet regularly for coffee to talk about what's going on in our lives, including our children, our relationships with our spouses, and our work. Talking through important issues with these friends helps me see new perspectives and inspires me to do what's right.

It's no coincidence that peer encouragement is a key element in 12-step programs such as Weight Watchers and Alcoholics Anonymous.[12] These programs have been very effective in helping people break bad habits. Peer encouragement helps people develop good habits too.

3. *Undertake periodic checkups.* Another, more formal way to become aware of blind spots is a 360-degree performance assessment. The review incorporates the feedback of people we report to and work alongside along with feedback from those individuals who report to us. It is an invaluable practice to gauge our strengths and development needs and to identify any blind spots. Critical to the effectiveness of this process is honest feedback. If people game

the system because they fear candid feedback will be met with retaliation, it will become a complete waste of time. The role of the primary evaluator (the person who summarizes and communicates the results) is especially important since he can work with those providing feedback to identify issues and communicate them in a way that will preserve their anonymity. For the more senior-ranking members of an organization, it may be advisable to bring in outside advisors to conduct the assessments. Annual 360-degree reviews are ideal although greater frequency will be necessary if an individual's development needs require rapid improvement.

4. *Study and celebrate the character of intentional connectors.* During the spring of 2002, I attended a conference in Washington, D.C., that featured David McCullough, one of my favorite historians. In his speech about John Adams, McCullough pleaded with the audience to study history because it is so relevant to our lives today.

In the past I rarely read about history. Inspired by McCullough's speech, however, I decided to read his best-selling book *John Adams.* To my surprise, I couldn't put it down. The accounts of Adams's life, his courage and determination, and his struggles made me think about my life. Next, I read the biographies of many of America's other founders. Then I began reading about a wide range of people I admired, including leaders of nations, armies, businesses, and sports teams, and thought leaders such Harriett Beecher Stowe and Mahatma Gandhi. Their life stories made me more determined to develop my character.

In the past, character was often taught through the transmission of oral and written stories. Public libraries are filled with books that teach us about character and encourage us in our character development. Today they are available in compact disc and downloadable file format for the person who prefers listening over reading.[13] Make it a point to learn about the stories of great men and women of the past and present. You won't be disappointed.

5. *Select, measure, and promote leaders who have character strengths and who connect.* Clearly this is something you will aspire to. Sometimes, however, your best performers are less than sensitive to others, and they expect special treatment because they know they are talented in some respects. When the negative effect of disconnection on the rest of the team is taken into consideration, it is not worth applying different standards to these leaders. The character strengths or weaknesses of leaders often ripple across an association of people to good or ill effect. A leader's character has a disproportionate impact because people look to leaders for guidance. That's why organizations would do well to establish processes that select people, especially leaders, with character strengths. Tests that assess personality attributes are useful for this purpose and also for identifying leaders who would benefit from coaching. The Ritz-Carlton Hotel Company administers a personality assessment to potential employees. Years of experience have taught the company which personality attributes are present in their best employees.

In addition to the 360-degree performance assessment, a periodic measurement of the degree of connection between leaders and their direct reports is important. An employee engagement survey that indicates engagement and connection have declined provides an early warning system that intervention may be required, including coaching or training. Employee engagement surveys are typically excellent for this purpose. Employee satisfaction surveys, however, are generally less effective because they fail to measure emotional connection.

6. *Consider insights and solutions that emerge from social network analysis.* Another useful tool to identify connection (and ultimately character) issues is a social network analysis. This framework attempts to understand the flow of information throughout an organization by surveying members about whom they communicate with and what they communicate about. The results are then aggregated and mapped to pinpoint key patterns and participants. Karen Stephenson, a leading thinker in the field, categorizes information flows into six networks: the work network, the social network, the innovation network, the expert knowledge network, the career guidance or strategic network, and the learning network. Within each network, Stephenson describes people as "hubs," "pulsetakers," and "gatekeepers."

Social network analysis identifies people who are key disseminators of knowledge and thus more valuable to the organization. Equally important, it detects people who are bottlenecks to the flow of information, thus reducing organizational effectiveness.

Social network analysis has also been used to design work spaces that maximize the dissemination of knowledge. For example, a person who serves as a hub and requires input from a broad network can be stationed near an area where people regularly congregate, such as a break area. People whose work is less social in nature can be situated in areas where fewer people congregate. By understanding the communication flows and physically locating people in areas to optimize connection where it is most needed, the organization will increase the likelihood that connection will occur and have a favorable impact on the organization.[14]

7. *Be careful not to develop a self-righteous culture.* The danger of focusing on character is that it can create a culture of legalism and self-righteousness. Mark Twain alluded to this when he

described some people as "good in the worst sense of the word." Any culture that encourages people to develop character must be on guard to assure that the character strengths of forgiveness, mercy, and humility are not lost in the desire to improve other aspects of character. Character strengths are goals for us to aspire to achieve. In reality, however, we all will fail periodically to live up to our character aspirations.

Forgiveness, mercy, and compassion should also be extended to those who lapse into moments of self-righteousness. It can happen to the best of us. The problem arises when a leader consistently demonstrates that he lacks the self-knowledge that produces compassion and empathy for others. It is this type of habitually self-righteous leader who should not be in a position of leadership.

Now that we have more fully explored the three elements of a connection culture—inspiring identity, human value, and knowledge flow—and the character strengths that support them, let's learn about twenty leaders and see how they increased connection and fired up people.

Review, Reflection, and Application

- ❑ Leading psychologist-scholars believe that individuals are mentally and physically healthier when they exhibit behavior that is consistent with twenty-four universally recognized character strengths.

- ❑ We must all develop habits that reflect character strengths and increase connection with others.

- ❑ We need high-trust relationships to help us see our blind spots and encourage us to develop our character.
- ❑ We also need periodic checkups, such as 360-degree performance reviews, to identify our blind spots.

- ❑ Learning the stories of intentional connectors encourages us to develop our own character.

- ❑ Organizations should select, measure, and promote leaders who have character strengths and who connect with others.

- ❑ Social network analysis can be a useful tool to identify information flows and the people who are integral to maintainingconnections, and to design work spaces to optimize connection.

- ❑ Be on guard not to develop a self-righteous culture. Instead, be certain that your culture values the character strengths of forgiveness, mercy, and humility.

- ❑ So what? To develop and maintain character strengths is well worth the effort. You need to develop your character and help those for whom you are responsible to develop their character. With 360-degree performance assessments, employee engagement surveys, and social network analysis you can identify people who increase and decrease connection and understand how work space might be designed to encourage connection.

PART IV

Learn from Twenty Great Leaders Over Twenty Days

In Part IV you will learn about twenty great leaders from various fields who fired up people by increasing connection. In some examples you will see a leader who relied primarily on one element of a connection culture to increase connection, whereas in other examples you will see a leader who relied on all three elements. Following each example, you will find a summary of some practices that increased connection as well as a question or two that ask you to consider how you might apply their practices in your organization.

The stories are arranged so that you can read one each business day and complete all of them over the course of one month. Or you can take them at a pace that works best for you. In the spirit of knowledge flow, you might find it helpful to meet with other readers to discuss the stories and compare your answers about how to apply the practices illustrated. Regardless of your approach, I hope you reflect on how the practices of these leaders might apply to your life.

WEEK 1

Day 1: French Hero of the American Revolution

Visiting historical sites in the state of Virginia, you might be surprised to see recurring tributes to a Frenchman whose name and story remain unknown to most Americans today. At Monticello, Thomas Jefferson's hilltop home near Charlottesville, you'll find a portrait and sculpted bust of the Frenchman. At Mount Vernon, George Washington's home on the Potomac River, you'll learn that Washington thought of him as a son, and you will find the key to the Bastille on display, sent by the Frenchman to Washington after he ordered the notorious Paris prison torn down during the French Revolution. Perhaps most surprising of all, in the Hall of Presidents beneath the rotunda of the Virginia capitol where a statue of George Washington and busts of the other seven Virginia-born presidents reside, you'll find a bust of the Frenchman who was neither a president nor born in Virginia.

Across America hundreds of landmarks are named after him. Every year on Independence Day, the American ambassador to France travels to his gravesite in Paris to replace the American flag that flies over it. The gravesite is unusual in France for the Frenchman's casket and that of his wife lie beneath soil taken from Bunker Hill outside Boston, Massachusetts, the site of one of the first battles in the Revolutionary War.

As you might guess, this Frenchman was far from ordinary. His name is Marie-Joseph-Paul-Yves-Gilbert du Motier de La Fayette, more commonly known as the Marquis de Lafayette.

Lafayette was one of the wealthiest young men in France. His early life was not an easy one. His father, a colonel of grenadiers, was killed in battle when Lafayette was two years old, and his mother and grandfather died when he was twelve. By fourteen he had joined the Royal Army, and at sixteen he married Marie-Adrienne-Françoise de Noailles, a wealthy relative of the French king.

In his late teens Lafayette became enamored with the cause of American independence. At a dinner he attended, Lafayette heard the Duke of Gloucester, a brother of England's King George III, share his strong opposition to the English treatment of American colonists. It seems from that point, Lafayette developed a consuming desire to see the American colonists achieve their independence.

At nineteen Lafayette purchased a ship, named it the *Victoire,* and persuaded several French army officers to join him in helping the Americans. After he arrived in America, Lafayette approached John Hancock, head of the Continental Congress, and volunteered his services. In a letter to Hancock, Lafayette, like the signers of the Declaration of Independence, pledged his "life, his fortune, and his sacred honor" to American independence. Lafayette was inspired by America's cause, and his inspiration led him to make a commitment to do everything he possibly could to achieve it.

Lafayette was commissioned as a major general and eventually became an aide-de-camp to George Washington. Historian Arthur M. Schlesinger Jr. noted that Lafayette "distinguished himself militarily . . . was an essential actor in the successful plan to trap the British Army under General Cornwallis at Yorktown . . . [and became] an invaluable ally of the American minister to France, Thomas Jefferson."

Perhaps most important, when Lafayette went back to France to secure resources for the Americans, he returned with an army of four thousand soldiers and a fleet of ships commanded by Count de Rochambeau. Before Lafayette's return, the American effort had been losing steam after suffering several defeats. Lafayette's presence, his infectious optimism, and the resources he brought revitalized the American effort.

Lafayette had a profound effect on the American military's culture during the Revolutionary War. He increased inspiring identity. He encouraged everyone around him by reiterating how important the war was for the future of humankind. Later in life he would comment: "To have participated in the toils and perils of the unspotted struggle for independence . . . the foundation of the American era of a new social order . . . has been the pride, the encouragement, the support of [my] long and eventful life."

Lafayette increased human value in many ways. He spent considerable personal wealth to purchase shoes and clothes for the men in his command. Although he could afford to buy a house to stay warm, he chose to remain with the soldiers at Valley Forge during the freezing winter of 1778. He fought alongside the infantrymen, even dismounting his horse if necessary to be closer to them. Lafayette treated soldiers with respect.

Lafayette increased knowledge flow by seeking the opinions of his soldiers, asking them what worked and what didn't work in the battles they had fought. He later claimed that the common soldiers were his greatest teachers. The soldiers were so fond of Lafayette that they referred to him as "Our Marquis."

The unlikely story of the French aristocrat fighting with dedication for their behalf endeared Lafayette to Americans everywhere. Author Harlow Giles Unger described it well when he said, "[Lafayette] fled from incomparable luxury . . . to wade through the South Carolina swamps, freeze at Valley Forge, and ride through the stifling summer heat of Virginia—as an unpaid volunteer, fighting and bleeding for liberty, in a land not his own, for a people not his own."[1]

For the Marquis de Lafayette's extraordinary commitment to America's cause, America passed a law on January 23, 2002, posthumously bestowing him with honorary citizenship. Only five other individuals in America's history have been honored in this way.

Application

Lafayette increased inspiring identity by reminding people of the importance of the Revolutionary War to the future of humankind. He increased human value by fighting beside the soldiers he commanded and suffering alongside them during the winter at Valley Forge. Lafayette increased knowledge flow by seeking the opinions of soldiers and considering their ideas. If you had been a soldier under Lafayette's command, which of these actions would have resonated with you the most? How can you make them resonate with your colleagues?

Day 2: Restoring the Glory

Anne Mulcahy, after being appointed the CEO of Xerox and bringing herself up to speed on the company's situation, shocked Wall Street by announcing Xerox's business model was unsustainable. Her remark caused Xerox stock to drop 26 percent the following day.

Despite her realization that Xerox had serious problems, she knew from her twenty-seven years at the firm that it could be revived. Although Xerox's outside legal and financial advisors recommended that the firm file for Chapter 11 bankruptcy protection, Mulcahy refused to because she knew it would discourage Xerox employees and make a turnaround even more difficult. She was determined to lead Xerox back to health. One colleague observed that her passion and work ethic were driven by her mission to save Xerox. To that effect, Mulcahy once said, "If this place is going to fail, it's not going to be because Anne Mulcahy slept."

Mulcahy's words and deeds effectively created an inspiring identity for Xerox that might be described as "restoring the glory." Her optimism and energy persuaded others that it could be done. And what a story it would be to revitalize a once great company. Who wouldn't want to play a part in that?

Another element in the Xerox culture created by Mulcahy was human value. Her comments showed she cared about the people she was responsible for leading. In a remarkably candid interview with *Fortune's* Betsy Morris in 2003, Mulcahy stated she would wake up some nights thinking about what would happen to the 96,000 employees who were counting on her if she failed to save the firm. And when, to keep Xerox afloat she had to shut down a business she had created and lay off many of the people she hired, Mulcahy went to meet them face-to-face. She told them she was sorry, that it had to be done to save the company, and that it wasn't their fault. Mulcahy made the tough decision and carried it out in a way that preserved the dignity of the people involved.

She also increased knowledge flow at Xerox. Mulcahy visited with fifty CEOs of client companies and boosted employee morale by logging one hundred thousand miles to visit Xerox employees in her first year. She encouraged people to tell her the truth, and she listened to them too. According to one of her colleagues, she "told us everything, stuff we didn't want to know . . . [like how close we were to running out of cash]." Another colleague remarked, "Part of her DNA is to tell you the good, the bad, and the ugly."

She asked them to be committed to the turnaround: "Save every dollar as if it were your own." And she rewarded those who remained at Xerox by refusing to eliminate raises and by extending small perks such as time off from work on their birthdays. She allowed Xerox's top hundred executives to have greater access to her, and she involved them in major decisions. As a result, ninety-five of them remained with Xerox throughout the turnaround.

One observer noted, "She was leading by example. Everyone at Xerox knew she was working hard and that she was working hard for them." The press accounts of Anne Mulcahy's heroic efforts had to encourage her colleagues. *Fortune* reported that she hadn't had a weekend off in two years, frequently visited three cities a day, carried her own luggage on flights, and did more cooking on the Xerox corporate jet than she had at her own home. During this critical stage to Xerox's survival and for a season in her life, Mulcahy was clearly making a personal sacrifice for the sake of the mission and her Xerox colleagues.

Mulcahy's optimism and hard work paid off. When she was named Xerox's CEO in May 2000, the firm was on the verge of bankruptcy and its stock had dropped from $63.69 a share to $4.43. After she took charge, Xerox employees rallied to support her. Thanks to leadership that strengthened connection among the people at Xerox, together they restored the company to profitability and positioned it for future growth, leading observers like Xerox board member and former CEO of Time Warner Nick Nicholas to proclaim, "The story here is a minor miracle."[1]

Application

Anne Mulcahy increased inspiring identity by holding out a vision of Xerox as a turnaround story and working hard to achieve it. She increased human value by being there with employees to console them when they lost their jobs. She increased knowledge flow by meeting with employees worldwide and hearing their ideas and concerns. If you were leading a turnaround situation, which of the means that Anne Mulcahy used to increase connection would you focus on, and why?

Day 3: The Shot Heard Around the World

When the Chicago Bulls NBA team is mentioned, chances are, the first person you think of is Michael Jordan. What sports fan wasn't inspired by arguably the game's greatest player ever? His last-second jump shots, airborne dunks, and tenacious defensive coverage made him a crowd-pleasing favorite.

When Michael Jordan began playing in the NBA, he epitomized excellence as an individual contributor. His superhuman feats during his first five seasons, however, were not enough to make champions out of the Bulls. Not until Phil Jackson became head coach and began to influence the young superstar did the Bulls finally make it to the big game.

Jackson helped Jordan see the need to go beyond being a star and become what Jackson called a player "who surrenders the me for the we." In the context of the Bulls this meant every individual playing as a team within the triangle offense that Jackson taught.

Until that time Jordan felt he needed to win games on his

own because he didn't have confidence that his teammates would perform in the clutch. But a one-man show, even if it was a show put on by one of the game's greatest players, was never going to be enough to get the Bulls to the top. Furthermore, Jordan spent little time with his teammates and instead hung out with his entourage that followed him around on the road. Jordan's self-reliance and social separation from his teammates made them feel like supporting actors on the Michael Jordan show.

Phil Jackson could see the problem. So he went to Jordan and convinced him that the team needed his leadership, which would require his presence and effort to get to know his teammates personally. Having Jordan present with the team would increase human value in the Bulls's culture. Jordan's presence and the trust he would put in his teammates would show he valued them as basketball players and as people.

Convinced that Jackson was right, Jordan transformed himself into a force for connection. He began spending more time with his teammates on and off the court. Writing about the experience in his book *Sacred Hoops,* Phil Jackson observed: "Jordan's presence [affected] the psyche of the team . . . he challenged everyone to step up . . . before practice I often found him working one-on-one with young players."

Connection was increased as Phil Jackson increased knowledge flow. His philosophy is that "I like everyone to feel that they have a seat at the table." Jackson knows that keeping people informed and listening to their viewpoints keeps them feeling connected.

The Bulls's inspiring identity was increased as Jordan and Jackson worked together to convince the other Bulls players that they were a team that deserved the world championship. Jordan and Scottie Pippen pushed the team to reach a new level of physical conditioning and preparation, which reinforced the players' beliefs that no team worked as hard or deserved a world championship more than they did.

Connection was also a part of the Bulls's identity. Jackson encouraged his members' commitment to the team by quoting a passage from Rudyard Kipling's *The Second Jungle Book.* The quote describes the law of the jungle: ". . . the strength of the pack is the Wolf. And the strength of the Wolf is the pack."

Jackson's Chicago Bulls team accepted his philosophy of teamwork as a path to basketball greatness. As connection among the team improved, the Bulls's success rose to a new level. Beginning in 1991 when the Bulls won their first world championship, Jordan's teammates sometimes made dramatic contributions to the games. In the past, when the score was close at the end of a game, Jordan always wanted the ball. After Jackson worked with Jordan, he trusted his teammates to make the big play during several pivotal situations.

One such instance occurred in game six of the 1993 championship when the Bulls played the Phoenix Suns. Near the end of the game, down by a score of 98 to 96, the Bulls came downcourt, and instead of passing the ball to Jordan, the Bulls got the ball to John Paxson, who shot and scored a three-point jumper just before the buzzer went off to win the game. The press hailed it as "the shot heard around the world." The following year in the final championship game against the Utah Jazz, Jordan passed the ball to his teammate Steve Kerr who hit a jump shot just before the buzzer to clinch another championship for the Bulls. Over the course of eight years, the Chicago Bulls won an astounding six world championship titles.

Michael Jordan went on to become a basketball legend for his performance as a player and as a part of a basketball dynasty. At the time of his departure from coaching the Los Angeles Lakers in

2004, Phil Jackson had a career record of 832 wins and 316 losses (a .725 winning percentage), making him the coach with the best winning percentage in NBA history. Between coaching the Bulls and the Lakers, Jackson won nine NBA championships.[1]

One key to Phil Jackson's success was that he challenged his players to become a team by putting the team first. Michael Jordan responded by humbly making a personal commitment to his team and teammates rather than continuing as a one-man show to the detriment of his team's performance. The resulting connection among the team and the performance that it made possible was the catalyst that transformed Jordan from being a great player into becoming a basketball legend. Ironically, the selfishness of some of Jackson's players on the Lakers team kept him from developing another basketball dynasty in Los Angeles during his first stint as head coach there. Now that Jackson has returned to the Lakers, his players are beginning to see the light. It may be that a second dynasty is in the making for Phil Jackson.

Application

Michael Jordan increased inspiring identity by sharing his belief with his teammates that the Bulls could become world champions and by personally working hard to achieve it. He increased human value by getting to know his teammates and taking the time to mentor younger players. Coach Phil Jackson increased knowledge flow by letting everyone know they had a seat at the table to share his ideas. Have you played on a team, or can you think of another team, that came together like the Bulls did? Is there someone in your organization that you could encourage or mentor?

Day 4: Soldier of Peace

George C. Marshall was one of the most extraordinary individuals to have lived during the twentieth century. Born in Uniontown, Pennsylvania, in 1880 and trained at the Virginia Military Institute, Marshall was a career military man who will forever be remembered for his efforts to promote peace and bring about a strong connection between America and Western Europe.

Reading the comments of Marshall's many admirers is awe-inspiring. Winston Churchill called Marshall "the true organizer of victory" for his efforts during World War II as army chief of staff for President Franklin Delano Roosevelt. The British chiefs of staff sent Marshall a message that read, in part, "Your name will be honoured among those of the greatest soldiers of your own or any other country . . . Always you have honoured us by your frankness, charmed us by your courtesy, and inspired us by your singleness of purpose and selfless devotion to our common cause." President Harry S. Truman said Marshall was "the greatest military man this country has ever produced—or any other country for that matter . . . the more I see and talk with him, the more certain I am he is the great one of the age." *Time* magazine named him Man of the Year twice.

As army chief of staff during World War II, Marshall was credited for building America's underprepared military infrastructure so that it would be in a position to win the war. After Marshall recognized that America was falling seriously behind Germany in military preparedness, though it would be another three years before America was attacked, he worked incessantly to revitalize American military strength. The energy and effort Marshall put into his work led Senator Henry Stimson to say, "I have never seen a task of such magnitude performed by a man."

Throughout his remarkable career, Marshall's actions encouraged connection among people. He increased human value in several ways. When FDR put the Civilian Conservation Corps during the Depression under Marshall's command, he developed an "absorbing interest" in helping the young men by educating them and taking care of their health-care needs. According to Marshall's biographer, he "kept his men intelligently occupied . . . giving them tasks that would awaken their interests." Married soldiers and their families suffered real economic hardship during the Depression so Marshall started a program that allowed every military family to pay only fifteen cents a meal. To avoid the perception that the program was a "condescending charity," he and Mrs. Marshall ate the meals too.

One of the best-known examples of Marshall's passion for human value was celebrated in the movie *Saving Private Ryan* that starred actor Tom Hanks. After learning that James Ryan's mother had lost three of her four sons in battle, Marshall sent a squad to France specifically to retrieve Private Ryan and return him to America and to his mother.

Perhaps the greatest example of Marshall's increasing human value came after World War II when President Truman asked Marshall to become secretary of state. He accepted the role because he envisioned the opportunity to remove the causes that led to war. For two years he set about to persuade Congress and the American people of the need to provide assistance to the war-torn economies of Europe where famine and disease were rapidly spreading. That was no easy task, considering the human inclination to avenge former enemies rather than help them. To his credit, Marshall knew that ignoring human suffering was wrong and would lead to bitter resentment and potentially to a future war. During a commencement speech at Harvard, General Marshall told the world: "Our policy is directed not against any country or doctrine but against hunger, desperation, and chaos." Marshall redirected his tireless efforts from waging a war to helping the very nations he had fought against. The Marshall Plan, as the reconstruction effort became known, was an overwhelming success. You can still visit European towns where merchants sell postcards that show the destruction following World War II, in stark contrast to the beauty of these same towns today.

For his humanitarian actions, he was the first career soldier to be awarded the Nobel Peace Prize in 1953. The British were so moved by the compassion and efforts of Marshall that when he entered Westminster Cathedral to attend Queen Elizabeth II's coronation and people in attendance spotted him, they stood in his honor.

George Marshall also increased knowledge flow in cultures by speaking truth to those in power. During World War I in France, General John "Blackjack" Pershing once criticized then Major Marshall's division commander in front of his subordinates over a mixup that was actually the fault of Pershing's office. As Pershing tried to walk away, Marshall refused to let him leave, even grabbing his arm to stop him, until Pershing heard the truth. The officers present thought Marshall's behavior would surely end his career. To Pershing's credit, however, he appreciated Marshall's candor and courage. Eventually, Pershing promoted Marshall to colonel, making him a part of his personal staff, and later promoted him to become his personal aide.

Another incident shows Marshall's commitment to openness and honesty. Years later when Marshall was attending his first conference with FDR, the president asked for his opinion on a subject that everyone else in the room had already agreed on. To the president's surprise, Marshall opined, "I'm sorry, Mr. President, I don't agree with you at all." Somewhat surprised, FDR abruptly ended the meeting. Afterward, Treasury Secretary Henry Morgenthau approached Marshall and said, "Well, it's been nice knowing you." As it turned out, FDR appreciated Marshall's integrity and his willingness to say what he really believed. A little over a year later, FDR made Marshall the army chief of staff reporting directly to him.

George Marshall increased knowledge flow by valuing education. One theme running throughout his career was an "insatiable desire to learn, to know, [and] to understand." Stationed in Tientsin, "he . . . [became] an authority on Chinese civilization, history, and language . . . [and was] the only American officer who could examine Chinese witnesses without the aid of interpreters." Marshall's awareness that Hitler was building a huge military industrial complex led him to warn of the Nazi threat and America's vulnerability.

The inspiring identity that George Marshall spread to others was one of a dutiful public servant to a worthy country that he loved. When the time arrived for the Allies to invade Europe, General Marshall had hoped to be the one to lead the effort as Supreme Commander of the Allied Forces. The position would be based in Great Britain. FDR, however, felt he needed General Marshall with him in Washington, D.C. Although he was personally disappointed, Marshall remained working for the president as army chief of staff and appointed Dwight D. Eisenhower to the position of supreme commander of Operation Overlord. While Marshall served in a less visible but nonetheless important role, Eisenhower's success as supreme commander served as a springboard to the presidency. It takes an extraordinary personal sense of one's duty for someone to make a sacrifice of the magnitude made by General Marshall.

George Marshall once said, "The less you agree with the policies of your superiors, the more energy you must direct to their accomplishment." This attitude gave FDR confidence that he could always count on Marshall, and the president expressed this confidence by saying, "When I disapprove [of Marshall's recommendations], I don't have to look over my shoulder to see which way he is going . . . I know he is going . . . to give me the most loyal support as chief of staff that any president could wish."[1] It takes an uncommon degree of integrity and humility to do this.

A soldier of peace, George C. Marshall left as a legacy strengthened connections among the peace-loving nations. His work laid the foundation for the unprecedented spread of liberty in the last half of the twentieth century.

Application

General George C. Marshall increased inspiring identity by becoming a role model of a soldier-statesman who was dedicated to his country and worked hard to do his best in the positions he held. He increased human value by standing up to General Pershing and defending the men in his command when he felt they were treated unfairly. General Marshall increased knowledge flow by learning what was going on outside America so that he could be prepared to respond to external developments. What qualities of George Marshall do you see in yourself? FDR said of Marshall, "I don't have to look over my shoulder to see which way he is going . . . I know he is going . . . to give me the most loyal support as chief of staff that any president could wish." Would your supervisor say the same about you?

Day 5: Hug Your Customers™

Mitchells/Richards/Marshs is a retail store phenomenon. In 2002, the leading menswear retailing magazine named the company Retailer of the Year. Its two locations in Greenwich and Westport, Connecticut, about an hour's drive from New York City, sell an astounding $65 million in clothing annually. Remarkably, half the households in those towns have purchased from the company. The company's clients include many well-known celebrities such as the actor Paul Newman and *Today Show* host Matt Lauer, as well as the last three CEOs of General Electric and the heads of IBM, Xerox, Starwood, PepsiCo, JP Morgan, Lehman Brothers, and many others. Most recently, the firm acquired Marshs in nearby Huntington, New York.

Surely near the top of the list of factors contributing to its success is the culture of Mitchells/Richards/Marshs, which revolves around connection. Mitchells/Richards/Marshs' management, employees, customers, and suppliers benefit from the strong connection that exists among them.

Connection has always been the foundation of Mitchells/Richards/Marshs. In 1958, Ed Mitchell traded an unfulfilling marketing and advertising career in New York City that was giving him ulcers for the world of retail. Ed and his wife, Norma, thought that opening a men's clothing store in Westport would allow them to do what they loved, which was connecting with people. They founded the store based on the belief that it was right to treat employees like family and customers like friends. Until he died in January 2004 at the age of ninety-eight, Ed continued to work at the Westport store several hours each week. Norma, too, had worked at the store up until her death a decade earlier. Retiring seemed out of the question to these two who loved connection.

Ed Mitchell's philosophy is enthusiastically embraced by his sons, Jack, now the company's CEO, and Bill, the vice chairman. Both men embody their father's love of people. Bill frequently reminds everyone that "it's just right to care for people." Jack is an energetic, warm-hearted leader who is a natural-born optimist and encourager. He and Bill are constantly on the move in both stores, making connections with customers and colleagues.

To bring the Mitchells' philosophy to life, Jack describes caring for people as giving them a metaphorical hug. He's even written about it in a best-selling book published in 2003, *Hug Your Customers: The Proven Way to Personalize Sales and Achieve Astounding Results.*

Inspiring identity is increased when leaders articulate a common cause that unites and inspires management and employees alike. Everyone who has a connection with Mitchells/Richards/Marshs is proud of what it stands for: a reputation for excellence as reflected in its first-class employees and high-quality clothing, a passion for caring about people, and a commitment to giving back to the community by regularly holding charity fund-raisers in its stores.

Human value pervades the Mitchells/Richards/Marshs culture. The leaders believe in getting to know associates and customers on a personal basis (and it's not uncommon for them to get to know their family members too). Managers make certain that employees have time for a life outside of work. They reach out to help associates in need (a bedside visit in the hospital or a homemade favorite dessert would not be unusual). Management is flexible to meet employee needs (such as letting a sixty-five-year-old employee take a nap during the middle of the day to restore his energy). Because they care about associates, there have been a few occasions when managers have told verbally abusive customers to take their business elsewhere.

Mitchells/Richards/Marshs wants customers to feel the stores are as welcoming as a home, so adults may enjoy a complimentary in-store espresso bar and children may wait in a comfortable television viewing area. Management and associates call customers and one another by their first names because that's what friends do. If a customer has an emergency after hours, they'll open up the store. Mitchells/Richards/Marshs' technology investments keep track of information on customers including their likes and dislikes.

They make it a practice to travel to their suppliers' headquarters because it shows they value them, and it's easier to connect with people when you meet them face-to-face. Anyone working at Mitchells/Richards/Marshs who consistently behaves in a way that is at odds with human value is respectfully shown the door.

In 1995, Mitchells acquired Richards, the premier men's clothing store in nearby Greenwich. Typically in acquisitions, management and employees of the acquirer exert an air of superiority toward management and employees of the acquired. This acquisition couldn't have been more different. Out of respect for their new colleagues at Richards, the Mitchells family maintained the Richards name and described the deal as a merger of equals, although it was technically an acquisition. They also maintained the salary-based compensation structure preferred by the Richards associates rather than force them to convert to the commission-based system used at Mitchells. Following the acquisition, Jack's sons, Russ and Bob, spent 80 percent of their time at Richards "hugging" their new colleagues to let them know just how much they were respected and appreciated. To this day, the Mitchells still refer to Ed Schachter, the former owner of Richards who continues to work at the store, as "the Boss."

Knowledge flow also increases connection at Mitchells/Richards/Marshs. By encouraging associates to express their opinions and ideas, management creates a stronger connection with them. In turn, associates consider each other's opinions and ideas, and the connection among them benefits the business. Management is intentional about hiring people who are listeners and learners who seek personal growth, believing these associates will naturally listen closely to customers and have valuable ideas and perspectives to share. Mitchells/Richards/Marshs creates a greater connection with customers by giving many top customers a voice via the company's client advisory board.

As Ed Mitchell knew from day one, and Mitchells/Richards/Marshs' success goes to show, connecting with people is not only the right thing to do, it's the wise thing to do too. And you can be sure Ed Mitchell's legacy of connecting with people is in good hands. Jack and Bill remain extremely active in the business, yet in many respects have passed the torch to the third generation. The family has unanimously designated Russ and Bob Mitchell co-presidents and future co-CEOs because "they are superhuggers" certain to maintain Mitchells/Richards/Marshs commitment to connection with employees, suppliers, and customers in the years ahead.[1]

Application

Mitchells/Richards/Marshs increased inspiring identity by clearly communicating its values of caring for people and holding high-profile fund-raisers in its stores for local charitable organizations. It increased human value by treating employees like family and customers like friends. Knowledge flow was increased at Mitchells/Richards/Marshs by hiring people who were good listeners and learners. What aspects of the Hug Your Customers™ philosophy would work in your organization?

WEEK 2

Day 6: A Most Unlikely Turnaround

One of the greatest turnaround stories in all of history is also one of the most unlikely. It is the story of Queen Elizabeth I, a twenty-five-year-old woman who inherited the throne of England in 1558 having no leadership experience, faced prejudice in a time when women were considered grossly inferior to men, and lived with frequent threats of death. Despite these obstacles, she overcame the odds and led her country from near financial ruin to one of the most powerful kingdoms on earth. She is a timeless example of how a leader can connect with people and bring out the best in them.

Elizabeth's start in life was far from auspicious. She was the daughter of King Henry VIII and Queen Anne Boleyn. When Elizabeth was two years old, the king accused her mother of adultery and had her beheaded in the Tower of London. At that time, Elizabeth lost her title as princess and her position in the line of succession to the throne. Some years later, however, her stepmother, Catherine Parr, persuaded King Henry to restore Elizabeth to the line of succession.

When Elizabeth became queen, England was unstable, and her chances of success, or even survival, looked dim. First, England was in a state of severe internal strife between Protestants and Catholics following the Reformation and Counter-Reformation. Second, its treasury was nearly empty. Finally, Pope Pius V had declared that "whoever sends [Queen Elizabeth] out of this world . . . not only does not sin but gains merit in the eyes of God." With the pope's blessing, plans to kill Elizabeth were hatched by groups in Rome, France, and Spain.

Despite the dire situation, Queen Elizabeth rose to the occasion. When word arrived that she had inherited the throne after her stepsister Queen Mary's death, Elizabeth slipped the queen's ring on her finger, kneeled, and declared Psalm 118:23: The Lord has done this, and it is marvelous in our eyes. With a sense of divine appointment, she set out on her long road to restoring England's glory.

What stands out about Elizabeth's reign is the strength of her commitment to her mission and her people. One sign of that commitment was her rejection of marriage to the love of her life, Robert Dudley. It was rumored that his terminally ill wife died from a fall that occurred when Dudley pushed her. If Elizabeth married Dudley, her leadership would have been compromised. She chose instead to declare herself "bound unto a husband which is the Kingdom of England . . . [and she would be pleased if she] lived and died a virgin."

Thereafter, Elizabeth became known as the Virgin Queen, a description that invited comparison to the Virgin Mary. The queen appears to have encouraged her new image. When Sir Walter Raleigh wanted to name a colony in North America in her honor, Elizabeth suggested the name Virginia.

Elizabeth met a military challenge in 1588. King Philip II of Spain had assembled the Great Armada of 130 ships and thirty thousand men to attack England and restore it to Catholicism. Elizabeth, intent upon leading her soldiers, personally went to Tilbury near the English Channel to join them and await the Spanish. Her soldiers were mesmerized, to say the least, as she circulated among them. One eyewitness described her as looking like a "sacred general." The speech she gave there has been described as "one of the greatest orations in British history." In part she said,

> My loving people . . . I am come . . . to live and die amongst you all. To lay down for God, my kingdom and for my people, my honour and my blood even in the dust. I know I have the body of a weak and feeble woman, but I have the heart and stomach of a King and a King of England too and think it foul scorn that . . . Spain or any Prince of Europe should dare to invade the borders of my realm; to which, rather than any dishonour shall grow by me, I myself will take up arms.

Although many of her subjects had come to adore her for her steadfast determination to make England great, it was at Tilbury, according to historian Simon Schama, that Elizabeth became a national icon. Fortunately, Elizabeth's readiness to fight was never tested. Before the Armada could arrive, a combination of the fast and maneuverable British ships with superior weaponry and the winds at sea devastated the Armada. The Spanish lost thirty ships and fifteen thousand men.

Inspiring identity was restored to England under Queen Elizabeth. Many historians agree that she was admired by her subjects, many of whom affectionately referred to her as "Good Queen Bess." Because the identity of the kingdom was so closely linked to the ruler's identity, the English people's affection for Queen Elizabeth and her growing stature in the world made them proud to be her subjects.

Elizabeth increased human value by demonstrating how she cared for people. When her advisors encouraged her to punish Catholics, she refused. She chose to dedicate herself wholly to her people rather than marry the man she loved, and she showed she was willing to fight alongside her soldiers. At a time when monarchs ruled with an iron hand, her actions showed compassion and a sense of obligation to her subjects.

Although knowledge flow was limited at this point in history, there is evidence that Queen Elizabeth listened to the advice of her closest advisors and carefully considered what she learned before making decisions. Because she was not as quick to rule on matters before her, or at least not as quick as past rulers, her critics decried her slower, more measured approach as evidence that she was a poor leader. In reality, Queen Elizabeth's thoughtful approach to making decisions served her and England well.

The increased connection among the English contributed to a revival of England's commercial and cultural activity. So successful was Queen Elizabeth's forty-four-year reign that it became known as England's Golden Age.[1]

Application

Queen Elizabeth I increased inspiring identity by declaring herself married to England as a sign of her commitment to her duty. She increased human value by refusing to punish Catholics who held views different from her own. She increased knowledge flow by listening to her advisors and considering their views. Are there times when you feel you need to work against the conventions of your time and bring about change? What themes in the Queen Elizabeth story inspire you?

Day 7: Enlightened Monarch?

As a young man, Prince Frederick II found himself in an unbearable situation. Living in the Prussian capital of Berlin in the early eighteenth century, Frederick longed for autonomy and independence but lived under an autocratic, overbearing father, Frederick I, the first king of Prussia. The king disapproved of Fredrick's more modern ways, so he beat and berated him publicly to force his son to comply with his wishes.

When the prince was eighteen years old, he and a friend were apprehended trying to escape to England. To punish his son, the king made Frederick watch as his friend was beheaded. Out of these harsh experiences Frederick learned what it felt like to be on the receiving end of a ruler who abused his power. Unfortunately, for the time being, there was nothing he could do about it. So he patiently waited for his hour to arrive.

In 1740, Frederick II assumed the Prussian throne. He seemed determined to lead in a far different way from that of his father. Influenced by the writings of John Locke and Cicero, he described himself as "the first servant of the state." His actions were truly revolutionary.

Prussia's inspiring identity increased with the spread of Frederick's image as an enlightened monarch. Under Frederick, Prussia saw its reputation grow as a European power, which also increased the cultural element of inspiring identity.

Frederick increased human value in several ways. He lived as an ascetic in modest accommodations compared to the grand palaces of most rulers. He established individual protections under law by expediting the legal process, abolishing torture, and making death sentences subject to his personal approval. He instituted the first German law code and educated judges, which led to Prussian courts gaining the reputation as the fairest courts in Europe. He set forth a policy of religious toleration. He rebuilt towns and thousands of miles of roads to connect communities. Knowledge flow increased when he protected freedom of the press and promoted education for his people.

The results of Frederick's rule were extraordinary. During the Seven Years' War, he successfully defended Prussia from French, Russian, and Austrian attacks, despite having fewer military resources. Ultimately, he built Prussia into one of the strongest states in Europe before he died in 1786.

Historian James MacGregor Burns called him "one of the most masterful . . . constructive and successful rulers in recent times." Voltaire, the French philosopher, described Frederick as "the Philosopher King." But his people called him the name by which he will forever be remembered: Frederick the Great.

Although Frederick realized remarkable success early in his reign, later on he began to fail as a leader. His insatiable desire for military conquest in order to achieve personal fame and meet his dead father's expectations overcame his desire to help the people. Eventually, the bloody battles Frederick undertook along with his sleeplessness and nightmares about his father contributed to his growing sense of hopelessness, despair, and poor health. As he aged, Frederick's behavior toward others became abusive. At one time he had the devotion of the Prussian people, but by the time of his death in 1786 few mourned him.[1]

APPLICATION

Frederick the Great increased the inspiring identity of Prussia by improving his reputation as an effective leader. He increased human value by making the law courts fair. He increased knowledge flow by improving education for Prussians. How might you change the conditions of your workplace environment after you have been promoted? What might you do differently than your supervisor?

Day 8: First in Their Hearts

Richard Neustadt, Presidential Scholar at Harvard University, observed the following about George Washington: "It wasn't his generalship that made him stand out . . . It was the way he attended to and stuck by his men. His soldiers knew that he respected and cared for them, and that he would share their severe hardships."

From the time he was a young man, George Washington kept a personal rule book to remind him of the behavior that he aspired to live out each day. Many of the rules embody human value and capture the respect and deference Washington showed for others throughout his life. Some entries read: "Every action done in company ought to be done with some sign of respect to those who are present"; "Speak not when you should hold your peace"; "Use no reproachful language against anyone"; "Submit your judgment to others with modesty"; "When another speaks, be attentive"; "Think before you speak"; and "Be not so desirous to overcome as not to give liberty to each one to deliver his opinion."

Like many other great leaders who inspire their followers, George Washington increased human value in the culture he was responsible for leading. The historian Edward G. Lengel described Washington's leadership during the extraordinarily cold winter of 1777–78 at Valley Forge as "sacrificial" and noted that "he took great care in seeing that his soldiers were well housed." Historian Henry Steele Commager noted Washington's sacrifice for America was supported by the facts that he served as commander of the Continental Army without pay and was nearly bankrupt by the time he returned home to Mount Vernon after serving as the country's first president. On one occasion when approached by soldiers who wanted to overthrow the wartime government and set up Washington to lead the country, he met with them and made it clear that the thought of overthrowing the colonial American government was repulsive to him and under no circumstances would he consider it.

When King George III of England heard the news that Washington resigned his military commission without seizing power following the American Revolution's conclusion, he was said to have commented, "If it is true, George Washington is the greatest man in the world."

The selfless behavior of Washington connected people with him as their leader because it promoted trust. When a leader demonstrates that he or she is leading for the sake of the mission and the people, rather than for self-serving purposes, people naturally become more trusting.

George Washington increased knowledge flow. He had a reputation for being quick to listen and slow to speak. During the Revolutionary War, Washington listened to the advice of his war council, a group of soldiers who reported directly to him, and their advice helped him avoid what would have been costly mistakes. During the Constitutional Convention over which he presided, Washington rarely said a word other than to intervene and make decisions to break a logjam in the deliberations.

Washington increased inspiring identity. He was committed to the cause of independence and frequently referred to it as "our glorious cause." His love of America and personal sacrifice for it inspired others. With all the brilliant individuals surrounding him—John Adams, Thomas Jefferson, Benjamin Franklin, Alexander Hamilton, and others—Washington was the one to whom they indisputably looked as the greatest leader among them.[1]

Under Washington's leadership and the culture he helped create, connection among the colonists united them to defeat the preeminent military power of their age and set the stage for a new nation to emerge.

Application

George Washington increased inspiring identity by telling the soldiers he led about their "glorious cause." He increased human value by sharing in the sacrifices that his soldiers made during difficult times. He increased knowledge flow by setting an example for others to be good listeners. Washington was one of the model leaders of our history. Can you think of a model leader in our time who inspires you? What qualities do you admire in that person or would you want to emulate in your work environment?

Day 9: Reconnecting a Nation

An extraordinary historical example of human value occurred following the bloody Civil War in America. It began when the head of the Confederate Army, General Robert E. Lee, met with the head of the Union Army, General Ulysses S. Grant, at Appomattox Courthouse in 1865 to negotiate the terms of the Confederate Army's surrender. General Grant demonstrated human value by allowing the Confederate officers to retain their swords, personal effects, and horses rather than require them to be surrendered to the Union Army. He also promised to return the horses of cavalrymen and artillerists who would need them for their small farms when they returned to civilian life. And finally, Grant provided food and water to Lee's troops who had eaten very little over recent days.

After the terms of surrender were finalized in a document signed by the two generals and it was time for Lee to depart, Grant accompanied Lee out the door. General Lee was beginning to mount his horse when Grant stepped back, stood at attention, and saluted him by raising his hat. Watching their commander, Grant's officers followed suit. Deeply touched by Grant's actions, General Lee turned and raised his hat respectfully to Grant and his officers as he departed.

Historically, victorious parties plundered their defeated enemies for economic gain and for revenge. As military men and graduates of the US Military Academy at West Point, Lee and Grant knew that Grant's actions were unusual—they exhibited the sense of respect and dignity implicit in human value. General Lee never forgot Grant's benevolence. Some years later, after he had become the president of Washington College in Lexington, Virginia, Lee heard a professor denigrate General Grant's character and shot back, "Sir, if you ever speak again disrespectfully of General Grant in my presence, either you or I will sever his connection with this university!"

Another act that increased human value in the post-Civil War culture occurred when President Abraham Lincoln called for magnanimity on the part of all Americans to heal the animosity between Northerners and Southerners. In his second inaugural speech Lincoln said,

> With malice toward none, with charity for all, with firmness in the right as God gives us to see the right, let us strive on to finish the work we are in, to bind up the nation's wounds, to care

> for him who shall have borne the battle and his widow and his orphan, to do all which may achieve and cherish a just and lasting peace among ourselves and with all nations.

The years following the Civil War were difficult for the South, but Robert E. Lee helped to bring about healing by setting an example for others. He swore allegiance to the United States and, as a result, brought tens of thousands of former Confederate soldiers back into the Union. On another occasion, General Lee led the way for white Southerners in an act that reverberated throughout America. At St. Paul's Episcopal Church in Richmond, Virginia, an African-American freedman stunned white parishioners by breaking tradition and being the first person to approach and kneel at the chancel rail to receive Communion. While other whites hesitated, the legendary general approached the rail and knelt beside the African-American man.[1]

These words and deeds of Grant, Lee, and Lincoln increased human value in America at a time when it was needed to reconnect its citizens.

Application

So often in mergers, some of the acquiring company's employees act superior to the employees of the acquired company. How did the respect that General Ulysses S. Grant and his officers showed to General Robert E. Lee increase human value, and how can employees of an acquiring company show a similar degree of respect toward employees of an acquired company? When you have been in a position of power, or as "victor," how have you treated the other side?

Day 10: Connection to the Cause

In 1852, a writer living in New Brunswick, Maine, published a book that would be a catalyst to abolish slavery in America. Her publisher was not optimistic that the book would sell many copies, nor was she.

They couldn't have been more wrong.

According to historian David McCullough, the book made publishing history, selling ten thousand copies in the first week and three hundred thousand in the first year. Three presses ran continuously to keep up with demand. Outside America the book sold one and a half million copies in a year and eventually was translated into thirty-seven languages. It is still being read, pondered, and discussed today.

McCullough observed this about the book:

> What the book did at the time was to bring slavery out into the open and show it for what it was, in human terms. No writer had done that before. Slavery had been argued over in the abstract, preached against as a moral issue, its evils whispered about in polite company. But the book made people feel what slavery was about.

The popularity of *Uncle Tom's Cabin* and its effect on readers took the author by surprise. Huge crowds came out to see her wherever she spoke. It was said that when President Abraham Lincoln met Harriett Beecher Stowe, he said, "So this is the little woman who made this big war." Pondering the power that written stories had on people, she wrote, "For good or for evil, [it] is a thing which ought most seriously to be reflected on. No one can fail to see that in our day it is becoming a very great agency."

On January 1, 1863, the day Lincoln signed the Emancipation Proclamation that freed slaves, Harriett Beecher Stowe was attending a concert in Boston. When someone in the crowd announced she was present, the audience gave her a standing ovation.[1]

Although Stowe was not a leader in the typical sense, she was clearly a thought leader. Slavery in America had been hotly debated and discussed since the founding of the country, and yet slavery was not abolished until more than eight decades after America achieved its independence. Stowe's words made it personal. Key to her success was her understanding of how Americans who were sympathetic to the abolition of slavery thought of themselves, in other words, their inspiring identity. Part of their inspiring identity was that they were decent, God-fearing people. The life of slavery described by Stowe was inconsistent with that identity. Likewise, they saw themselves as people who stood up against oppression. By writing a story that described conditions they deplored, Stowe forged an emotional connection among them that rallied them to make supreme sacrifices for the sake of their shared cause.

Application

With her book *Uncle Tom's Cabin,* Harriett Beecher Stowe touched the hearts of abolitionists. Her vivid description of the evils of slavery outraged those who thought of themselves as decent people and moved them to action. Would you have the courage to expose wrongdoing in your organization? How might you create awareness of a standard practice that you know is wrong?

WEEK 3

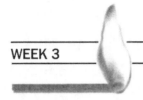

DAY 11: COMMUNITY CATALYST

In 1982, Howard Schultz, the current chairman and chief global strategist of Starbucks, left his prestigious job as national sales manager for a European housewares company to join a small, Seattle-based coffee roaster and retailer. Starbucks had come to Schultz's attention when he noticed the small business was purchasing a disproportionately large number of coffee makers from his company. When Schultz visited Seattle, he stopped to check out Starbucks and became intrigued with the possibilities. "I saw Starbucks, not for what it was but for what it could be," he said.

The key to Schultz's vision was simple: create community. The idea came to him while visiting Milan, Italy, where he observed people gathering at their neighborhood espresso bars "like an extension of the front porch, an extension of the home," he liked to say. At Starbucks, Schultz saw a means to bring people together in America, just as espresso bars bring them together in Italy.

Unfortunately, the founders of Starbucks didn't share Schultz's vision and preferred to remain a coffee roaster with a small retail presence. Schultz's belief in the idea, however, was so certain that he eventually left Starbucks in 1985 to start an espresso bar retailer. Two years later, he bought Starbucks from its owners and merged it into his small company. Schultz, a passionate, visionary leader, revolutionized coffee retailing in the USA and is rapidly taking Starbucks worldwide.

Howard Schultz carefully nurtured an inspiring identity for

the company in the hearts and minds of employees. At first he told his story and explained in detail how Starbucks would become an oasis for people as they took time out of their increasingly busy days to stop by for a brief period to relax. As the company grew by 1997 to more than 1,300 stores and 25,000 partners, it became impossible for Schultz to reach everyone in person. So he did the next best thing. He compiled his stories into an inspiring book titled *Pour Your Heart into It.*

Pour Your Heart into It is a compelling account of the Starbucks story. Every Starbucks partner who reads it will understand Starbucks's history and where it's headed. The book is filled with vividly told stories, including Schultz's vision for creating community. By articulating his vision, he transformed their work experience from selling coffee to a higher calling of creating community among people.

Schultz brought human value to the Starbucks culture by paying employees well relative to other retailers, and also providing generous benefits such as health-care insurance and participation in the Starbucks stock option plan.

Schultz increased knowledge flow in the Starbucks culture by making it everyone's responsibility to share ideas about how to continuously improve the business. Schultz presented a very approachable persona that made people comfortable that it was safe to be honest with him.

Fostering a connection between employees (or "partners," as they are known at Starbucks) and customers is an integral part of the Starbucks experience. Partners are trained to understand how to make a customer's visit true to Starbucks's mission (frontline employees' behavior is aligned with the mission to create community). Habits such as making eye contact with customers, remembering regular customers' drink orders, and anticipating customer needs are developed through orientation and ongoing training programs.

The results speak for themselves. By 2005, Starbucks had more than 100,000 partners, 10,801 retail locations, 35 million customers walking through its doors, and a record $6.4 billion in revenue during its fiscal year. Its success should come as no surprise given that Starbucks says, "The human connection . . . is the foundation of everything we do."[1]

Application

Howard Schultz increased inspiring identity by telling the Starbucks story in writing so that anyone could read it and understand how Starbucks developed its values. He increased human value by calling employees "partners" and compensating partners above industry norms. Shultz's approachable persona increased knowledge flow because he made it safe for people to be honest with him. Do you know the inspiring identity of your organization? Could you articulate it for yourself and others? Do you feel that everyone is on the same page?

Day 12: The Business of The Body Shop

In 1976, Anita Roddick, a thirty-three-year-old housewife, founded The Body Shop in Brighton, England, to support herself and her two daughters while her husband embarked on an expedition across the Americas. By the time he returned from the trip ten months later, she had opened a second location. Today, The Body Shop can be found in fifty-three countries, and it has grown to more than two thousand stores.

What contributed to The Body Shop's remarkable rise over the last thirty years? Certainly, several factors are responsible, including The Body Shop's culture that increases trust, cooperation, and esprit de corps among its employees.

Roddick gave The Body Shop an inspiring identity when she dedicated the organization to "the pursuit of social and environmental change." Roddick helped people connected to The Body Shop see how they could use their business to generate revenue that would be used in part to advance The Body Shop's values: eliminate animal testing, support community trade, defend human rights, activate self-esteem, and protect our planet. For example, community trade would be advanced when The Body Shop bought natural hair and skin care products from developing nations and sold them to customers around the world.

Defending human rights and protecting the environment could be advanced through The Body Shop's activities to educate customers, conserve resources in their day-to-day business, and organize protests against organizations or nations that behaved in a way that was counter to The Body Shop's values. The Body Shop's efforts to advance its values included everything from protesting against the Brazilian embassy in London over its cooperation with mining companies whose employees introduced diseases that threatened local tribes, to raising awareness and money to stop domestic violence.

Because the values of The Body Shop were values that Anita Roddick cared about, she became a tireless spokesperson and spiritual leader of the organization while her husband, Gordon, ran the day-to-day business operations. Anita was unconcerned about profit as long as it was sufficient to provide the resources to support The Body Shop's cause. Naturally, The Body Shop attracted employees who shared these values, and that common ground created a strong sense of connection among employees. When a reporter for *Inc.* magazine asked Roddick about the success of The Body Shop and particularly about the company's unusual dedication to its mission, she replied, "[A cause that grabs an employee's] imagination . . . produces . . . a sense of passion you simply won't find in [most other stores] . . . It's a way for people to bond to the company."

The Body Shop increased human value in its culture through employee training that emphasized the benefits of its natural products. The training was informational rather than lessons in ways to persuade potential customers to buy products.

Knowledge flow increased when Roddick created the company's popular in-house newspaper to communicate directly with the growing number of Body Shop employees around the world. It contains a mix of articles on the company's efforts to advance its mission of social and environmental change as well as poetry, facts about the environment, and educational stories. Several books that Roddick has written also increase knowledge flow.

In 2003, Anita Roddick became a Dame of the Order of the British Empire. In March 2006, L'Oreal agreed to purchase The Body Shop for £652 million (almost $1.14 billion US dollars). Dame Anita Roddick announced her intention to remain with The Body Shop as a consultant (the position she has held in recent years), and she reconfirmed that she would give her money to organizations that upheld The Body Shop's values.[1]

Application

Anita Roddick increased The Body Shop's inspiring identity by giving it a cause: the pursuit of social and environmental change.

She increased human value by training employees to understand The Body Shop's natural products and the benefits of using its products. Roddick's investment of her personal time and attention to communicate to employees through the company's popular newspaper increased knowledge flow. Do you feel inspired by the vision and values of your organization? Are you working toward a greater goal than just your day-to-day job?

Day 13: More Than an Oracle

Warren Buffett is widely recognized as an exceptional judge of corporate value. "The Oracle of Omaha," as he is known, is arguably the most successful investor in history. Corporate leaders from Jeffrey Immelt of General Electric to Martha Stewart make the trek to Omaha, Nebraska, seeking his wisdom. With so much attention on Buffett's investment acumen, it's easy to overlook another talent: motivating people. It's one of a host of reasons his investments tend to outperform the market.

The talented managers who run Buffett's companies remain with him because he keeps them engaged in their jobs. In Buffett's own words, "Charlie [Charlie Munger, Buffett's longtime business partner] and I mainly attend to capital allocation and the care and feeding of our key managers . . . Most of our managers are independently wealthy and it's up to us to create a climate that encourages them to choose working with Berkshire over golfing or fishing."

A closer look at Buffett shows, at least in part, how he does it.

He imparts an inspiring identity to members of the Berkshire Hathaway family. The vision he constantly communicates is that Berkshire companies are well managed and have great people. It's not unusual to hear him tell employees to "just keep on doing what you're doing . . . we're never going to tell a .400 hitter to change his batting stance." Who wouldn't be flattered to be praised by Buffett?

Buffett increases human value in several ways. He is trusting and forgiving. By investing for long periods in the companies he owns, Buffett indicates that he trusts his managers. He delegates decision-making authority, in his own words, "to the point of abdication." And when a manager makes an honest mistake, he keeps it in perspective. One manager who informed Buffett that his business had to write off $350 million was stunned when Buffett told him, "We all make mistakes . . . if you didn't make mistakes, you can't make decisions . . . You can't dwell on them."

He increases human value by modeling civility and respect for others. His secretary has said she hasn't seen him mad once in the nine years she has worked for him. The one time I met Buffett at a meeting in New York City, he patiently waited around to speak with everyone who wanted to meet him. He was attentive and focused on them, never projecting the slightest hint of self-importance.

He is confident, yet humble. Buffett knows he's very good at what he does, and he projects an easy confidence rather than superiority or arrogance. He credits his managers for his success, remains plain spoken, works in a modest office, lives in a modest house, and proclaims thrift as a virtue (the vanity plate on his car reads "Thrifty").

Compare Warren Buffett to Donald Trump, for example. It's hard to imagine Buffett prominently displaying his name all over everything he owns or relishing in telling someone "you're fired." Instead of everything being all about him, Buffett insists it's all about others. He appears to be guided by the Golden Rule rather than Machiavelli's *The Prince*.

Given the way Buffett treats people, it should come as no surprise that some private company owners report turning down more lucrative offers to join the Berkshire family. It is telling that no manager who sold a company to Buffett has ever left for a competitor, and several continue to work well into their eighties. Put simply, "people want to work for him," proclaimed another satisfied manager, Rich Santulli, head of NetJets.

Buffett increases knowledge flow by modeling approachability and candor. At the annual meeting he hosts in Omaha for Berkshire shareholders, Buffett and Charlie Munger sit on a platform, listening to shareholder opinions and answering questions for hours on end. In dealing with his managers he follows the data they provide him in periodic reports and makes himself available if they want to talk.[1] Buffett writes and speaks with candor, even pointing out mistakes he made and what he learned from them.

Leaders would be wise to emulate the way Warren Buffett leads Berkshire Hathaway. Perhaps we need a book on how the Oracle of Omaha inspires rather than yet another on how he invests.

APPLICATION

Warren Buffett increased inspiring identity by frequently praising the employees of companies owned by Berkshire Hathaway, referring to them as ".400 hitters." He increased human value by treating people with respect, giving them autonomy "to the point of abdication," and being quick to forgive them if they made an honest mistake. Buffett increased knowledge flow by personally being approachable and candid in his public comments. Imagine working at Berkshire Hathaway. How do you think you would feel? Is it very different from your current work environment? Is there anything you could do in your organization to bring about this kind of engagement?

Day 14: Ritz-Carlton Character and Culture

While I was working on this book my family spent several vacation days at the Ritz-Carlton Resort on Key Biscayne near Miami. I have long been a fan of the Ritz-Carlton Hotel Company, having stayed there during business trips over the years. I knew from firsthand experience that Ritz-Carlton connects with its guests. On this particular trip, I was determined to closely observe the employees to learn more about the best practices of the company.

One of the first Ritz-Carlton employees we met was Mery Castelblanco, a gracious, Colombian-born club concierge. Mery told us about the club and asked about our children. Immediately, Katie and I were impressed with Mery's focus on us and her kind, caring spirit. Throughout our stay, the club staff—Mery, supervisor Marc Rapp, concierge Paul Hoyo, and others—helped us line up activities for the week. With our frequent interactions, we learned more about their backgrounds and families, and they learned more about us.

My impression of the Ritz-Carlton staff was echoed by another guest, who remarked, "The people here are so nice." And she was right. Actually, Ritz-Carlton is intentional about hiring people who fit that general description. Marco Selva, the resort's general manager, graciously took time to sit down with me and discuss the company. He told me that Ritz-Carlton employees are selected based on a structured talent interview by telephone that identifies character strengths such as caring and empathy. In addition, potential employees undergo numerous interviews with current staff who provide feedback about whether they would want to work alongside a particular job candidate.

During our stay at the Ritz-Carlton, I couldn't help noticing how the guest experience reflects the cultural element of human value. For example, whenever I made eye contact with Ritz-Carlton employees—in an elevator, a hallway, or anywhere else for that matter—they always greeted me with a smile and a warm hello and wished me a pleasant day. They seemed to be looking for opportunities to go the extra mile. Early one morning I was returning to our room with cups of coffee for Katie and me when the floor's housekeeper noticed I had my hands full. Right away she set aside what she was doing and insisted on helping me. She walked with me to the room and opened the door with her room key so I wouldn't risk spilling our coffees. What's more, she seemed genuinely delighted to help me. It was a small act of kindness but one that I sincerely appreciated. On another occasion, when we wanted to pick up a certain DVD at the local Blockbuster to watch in our room but didn't have an account, our club concierge Paul Hoyo contacted Blockbuster and made the arrangements for us to use his personal account at the store. I could go on and on, but I'm certain you get the idea.

One secret to the Ritz-Carlton's success is that the organization takes good care of its employees. According to Sue Stephenson, Ritz-Carlton's head of human relations, guest and employee loyalty go hand in hand. That's why Ritz-Carlton is so particular about its workplace culture and disciplined in maintaining it. Its Employee Promise states unambiguously:

> At The Ritz-Carlton, our Ladies and Gentlemen are the most important resource in our service commitment to members and guests. By applying the principles of trust, honesty, respect,

> integrity and commitment, we nurture and maximize talent to the benefit of the individual and the organization. The Ritz-Carlton fosters a work environment where diversity is valued, quality of life is enhanced, individual aspirations are fulfilled, and The Ritz-Carlton mystique is strengthened.

The Ritz-Carlton's inspiring identity is reflected, first of all, in the employees' pride in the company's reputation for excellence. Employees are also united by the company's values that include treating everyone with dignity and respect, creating pride and joy in the workplace, continually identifying defects to be corrected, recording individual guest preferences in the firm's guest database, taking pride in and care of their personal appearance, using proper vocabulary, and so on. Each of the preceding values is represented in "The Ritz-Carlton Basics," a set of twenty values, one of which is reviewed each day during a brief session known as the Daily Lineup that supervisors have with their staff. By continuously reviewing this list of values, Ritz-Carlton keeps them on the minds of all staff. Each Monday the company's locations worldwide celebrate employees who went above and beyond the call of duty to serve a guest. When I met with Marco Selva, he happily recounted the story of Miriam Carballo, a receptionist at the front desk who overheard that a guest family's car seat had broken and gave them the car seat her child had outgrown.

At Ritz-Carlton, the cultural element of human value is reflected in several ways. Beginning on the first day of work, an employee goes through a two-day orientation led by the hotel's training manager. Each hotel's general manager participates in these sessions and interacts with the trainees. Each employee also receives training about his specific job and then recertification training annually for his position. Ritz-Carlton's employees have the right to be involved in planning work that affects them. The respect and dignity that Ritz-Carlton aims to provide its guests apply equally to its employees. Marco Selva told me he periodically asks disruptive or verbally abusive guests to go elsewhere and even arranges their transportation to a different hotel property at the Ritz-Carlton's expense. Emphasizing how much the Ritz-Carlton values its employees, he told me that "our employees respect that tremendously."

Knowledge flow is present in the Ritz-Carlton culture. Early in an employee's tenure she is asked to share her observations about how Ritz-Carlton can improve. Furthermore, Marco Selva and other general managers hold quarterly meetings with all employees to share performance results (including financial and ongoing guest-satisfaction survey results) and seek employee input. White boards are maintained on the walls in the various departments where ideas to improve are recorded for staff to see.

With the high degree of connection among management, employees, and guests, it should come as no surprise that Ritz-Carlton was the first and only hotel to win the prestigious Malcolm Baldrige National Quality Award and the only service company to win it twice. After all, the statement that "the genuine care and comfort of our members and guests is our highest mission" is more than words on paper at the Ritz-Carlton.[1] It's a way of life.

Application

Ritz-Carlton increases inspiring identity by upholding values that its employees personally embrace and by routinely celebrating employees whose actions embody those values. It increases human value by having guests leave if they become disruptive or verbally abusive to an employee. Knowledge flow is increased at Ritz-Carlton by maintaining white boards in the departments where employees can record ideas for improvements. What other "to-dos" could you put on your organization's list that would bring about this corporate cohesiveness? What ideas might come out of a brainstorming session in your organization?

Day 15: Peter Drucker's Kind of Leader

The preeminent management sage, the late Peter Drucker, knew some of the greatest leaders of our time in business and government. If he had been asked to name who he thought was a model leader, would he have chosen President Dwight D. Eisenhower, General George C. Marshall, the legendary Alfred P. Sloan Jr. of General Motors, or one of the many other heads of major companies throughout the world he came to know during his distinguished career? It's an interesting question, given the reach and influence of Drucker. Periodically in his interviews and writings you will encounter what may be his highest praise for a person who, he once said, "could manage any company in America." Who is she? *Business Week* featured her on its cover surrounded by . . . Girl Scouts. Her name is Frances Hesselbein.

Although she had no daughters, Frances Hesselbein began her association with the Girl Scouts when she agreed to help with a troop of thirty Girl Scouts in Johnstown, Pennsylvania, that had lost its leader. It wasn't long before Hesselbein's experience with Troop 17 developed into a lifelong commitment to Girl Scouting. Years later she would become CEO of the national organization, Girl Scouts of the USA.

Hesselbein increased the Girl Scouts' inspiring identity by showing women how important it was to reach out to girls, given the threats they face such as drugs and teen pregnancy. She helped women to envision the Girl Scout organization as a professional, well-managed organization.

Hesselbein's leadership style, in fact, it seems her purpose in life, is to bring out the best in the people she meets. Her words and actions embody human value. She has a high regard for people that shows she values them. She has written that good leaders have an "appreciation of their colleagues individually and the dignity of the work their colleagues do." Her actions show that she "walks the talk." She keeps up with what's going on in the lives of the people around her and personally reaches out to them when congratulations or consolation is in order. She invested in improving Girl Scout leaders' people skills. On her watch she built a conference center to train Girl Scout staff. Frances Hesselbein, as a role model for other leaders across the organization, effectively increased human value within the Girl Scout culture, and her actions were multiplied when other leaders adopted her leadership style.

The energetic leader increased knowledge flow by approaching communication in an inclusive way, expanding information in ever-larger circles across the organization. Rather than lecturing, her style is to ask insightful questions to draw out relevant issues. In planning and allocating the Girl Scout organization's resources, she introduced a circular management process that involved virtually everyone across the organization.

With Hesselbein as its leader, the Girl Scout organization thrived. When she assumed the CEO position in 1976, the Girl Scouts' membership was falling, and the organization was in a state of serious decline. She put sound management practices in place. During her twenty-four-year tenure, Girl Scout membership quadrupled to nearly three and a half million, diversity more than tripled, and the organization was transformed into what Drucker called "the best-managed organization around." Hesselbein accomplished the amazing turnaround with a paid staff of six thousand and 730,000 volunteers.

By the time she resigned from the Girl Scouts in 1990, the organization's future was bright. Frances Hesselbein was paid the ultimate compliment by Drucker when he recruited her to be the head of the Drucker Foundation (renamed the Leader to Leader Institute), which is dedicated to carrying out their mutual passion for strengthening leadership in the social sector.[2] It should be no surprise that the foundation's influence is rapidly growing worldwide with Hesselbein leading the effort. After all, the extraordinary Drucker, who lived to the age of ninety-five, knew a great leader when he saw one.

Application

Frances Hesselbein increased inspiring identity by helping Girl Scouts' staff see how important their work was to girls in today's world. She increased human value by reaching out to people across the organization to congratulate or console them. She increased knowledge flow by introducing a management process that intentionally involved practically everyone in the organization. As you move from authority to influence in leading people, particularly in a volunteer organization, the challenge of inspiring employees increases. How do the elements of inspiring identity, human value, and knowledge flow allow you to increase your influence and effectiveness?

Day 16: Dr. Fred's INN

In the medical profession, surgeons have a reputation for being task masters. Most surgeons stay focused on procedures and maintain a safe emotional distance from their colleagues and patients. In the mid-1990s, Dr. Fred Epstein, a world-famous pediatric neurosurgeon on staff at the prestigious New York University Medical Center in New York City, sensed something was wrong with this way of thinking. He became more convinced after he read a poem written by Chris Lambert, a seventeen-year-old patient who died from a malignant brain tumor. Chris wrote about his pain and struggle against disease and the fear of death. Dr. Epstein, or "Fred" as his patients and colleagues called him, adored this young man who was so full of life and had such a big heart. When Fred read Chris's poem and his plea for care and sympathy, it broke his heart.

Chris's words "demolished" Fred, according to his account in his book *If I Get to Five: What Children Can Teach Us About Courage and Character*. Although Fred had done everything he could to save Chris, he realized that he failed to respond to his young patient's plea to meet his deepest need: the need to connect on an emotional level. Chris's words made Fred wonder just how many kids he had failed in this way over the course of his long career. It also left him with a longing to change and a dream about what could be.

One afternoon, Fred received a call from the chairman of the board of trustees at Beth Israel Hospital in New York City. He offered Fred a blank check to create a new pediatric neuroscience center. Fred's vision became the inspiring identity of the Institute for Neurology and Neurosurgery (the INN). The INN would be a place where no patient would be turned away, regardless of medical situation or financial resources; where surgeons, nurses, and other health-care professionals collaborated and connected, and together they connected with patients and their families; and where the professionals no longer needed to separate their work and emotional lives.

In preparing to staff the INN, Fred didn't want to "persuade" people to join him. Instead, he found that when he shared his vision, the inspiring identity of a new kind of pediatric neurology and neurosurgery center that emphasized caring for the whole patient, the hearts of many of his colleagues were stirred. Like Fred, they yearned for a better way to care for their patients. To Fred's surprise, 108 highly trained doctors, nurses, and other health-care professionals followed him to work at the INN.

From the beginning, the INN's environment was created to connect people. Human value was increased in the INN's culture by reducing the degree of formality, making doctors and staff more approachable. White coats were banned. Doctors were addressed by their first names. Doctors, nurses, and other health-care professionals were encouraged to collaborate with one another rather than treat doctors as if they were better than everyone else.

Perhaps most important, everyone was encouraged to connect with colleagues, patients, and their families. Doctors, nurses, and other staff, including members of the cleaning crew, participated alongside families in interdenominational services, prayer circles, and physical therapy sessions such as massage and yoga. Everyone was free to take time to play games with the children or hold a child's hand during chemotherapy. Fred provided an excellent example for others to follow. He provided his home number to the families of patients. Fred and the INN's chaplain joined families if they wanted to pray prior to a child's surgery.

Human value increased when the young patients reached out to connect with and help one another or to encourage a parent. Mischa Zimmerman, a teenage patient at the INN who saw the positive impact of giving his *Toy Story* video to another young patient, founded the "Kids Helping Kids" program that encourages teens from schools in the greater New York City area to connect with teens facing health problems.

Knowledge flow increased because of the INN's informal culture. The embrace of collaboration also increased knowledge flow among staff.

After the first six years of the INN's existence, Fred realized: "My colleagues and I have reached a paradoxical conclusion: we've become better healers—more compassionate, more resilient, and more creative problem-solvers."

Over the course of his career, Dr. Fred Epstein created new surgical techniques and developed caring means to treat patients. Through his efforts, thousands of lives were saved, often the lives of patients that other doctors had deemed terminal. He published more than 175 scholarly papers, served as president of the International Society of Pediatric Neurosurgery and the American Society of Pediatric Surgeons, and was editor in chief of the *Journal of Pediatric Neurosurgery.*

In late 2001, when Dr. Epstein suffered a traumatic brain injury following a fall while on a Sunday morning bike ride near his home, his colleagues and former patients of the INN rallied to encourage him through his recovery. Although it was unlikely that he would perform surgery again, he continued to work at the INN, concentrating on fund-raising and advancing his vision to merge state-of-the-art medicine with a caring, healing environment.

On July 9, 2006, Dr. Epstein died from melanoma.[1] His family and thousands of patients, colleagues, and friends mourned him. Dr. Fred Epstein's example of compassion and courage will be long remembered.

Application

Dr. Fred Epstein increased inspiring identity by sharing his vision for a pediatric neurology and neurosurgery center that emphasized caring for the whole patient. He increased human value by removing the formal barriers—such as wearing white coats and using "doctor" titles—so that patients could more easily connect with doctors. He increased knowledge flow by getting the INN's staff to use first names when addressing one another rather than formal titles and treating each other as partners in curing illness. If you were given a blank check to create your own department or center, what elements would you incorporate? What would be important to you? What stops you from trying some of these today? Is it a question of money or the current culture of your organization?

Day 17: Purpose-Driven Pastor

In the summer of 2005, I was attending a session at the Aspen Institute, a think tank in Aspen, Colorado, when in walked a participant in the panel discussion about fifty of us had gathered to hear. If I could use only two words to describe this man, they would be *fun* and *unpretentious,* hardly adjectives you would expect to be used about one of the most influential religious leaders in the world today. Yet those were the words that came to mind as I watched Rick Warren, pastor of Saddleback Community Church in Orange County, California, and author of the best-selling *The Purpose-Driven Life.*

A big man, Warren was dressed in his trademark Hawaiian shirt that made him look as if he was more likely to be headed to a backyard barbeque than to speak at a conference that also featured former chairman of the Joint Chiefs of Staff and Secretary of State Colin Powell, AOL founder Steve Case, and PBS newsman Jim Lehrer. I noticed that they were also in the audience to hear Warren speak.

After briefly saying hello to the other panelists, Pastor Rick, as most people call him, began to make his way around the room to greet everyone in attendance, not just the famous people in the room but each one of us. It was clear from observing Pastor Rick that he was intentional about connecting with people. I shouldn't have been surprised, given the glowing accounts written by social commentator Malcolm Gladwell and Harvard social capital expert Robert Putnam about how Warren employs connection to expand Saddleback Community Church's ministry.

Today, twenty thousand people on average attend weekly services at the nondenominational Protestant church. Saddleback Community Church began in 1980 in a Bible study with seven people. One factor that helps explain Saddleback Community Church's growth is the connection that occurs through its small group ministry. In these groups, six or seven people meet weekly in each other's homes to study the Bible and support and encourage each other. In Orange County, where commutes to work are long and the gated subdivisions are not especially conducive to giving residents a sense of community, Saddleback Community Church's small groups help meet the human need for connection. The church's two hundred programs also create connection among people in the church's community.

Pastor Rick encourages connection when he speaks at church services. He teaches people to follow the biblical command to "love your neighbor as yourself," which increases human value. He encourages them to "seek the counsel of others" and "be quick to listen, slow to speak, and slow to become angry," both of which increase knowledge flow. Through the teaching of the church, a person in the Saddleback community becomes aware of the person (or the inspiring identity) that he should become.

Saddleback Community Church's ministry reaches people around the world through its Web site Pastors.com that provides resources such as sermon material and sources of encouragement to ministers. On the average day, Pastors.com gets approximately four hundred thousand hits. It clearly connects with pastors.

The phenomenal success of *The Purpose-Driven Life* put Rick Warren and Saddleback Community Church in the national spotlight. The book is designed to take a small group of people through a forty-day course to help them grow spiritually. It was launched by preselling copies at a discount to Pastor Rick's network of pastors, who bought stacks of them for their church members. The book presold a half million copies and began selling at a half million a month.

The book royalties alone could have made Pastor Rick and his wife, Kay, extremely wealthy (which might have alienated him from some in his church and his Pastors.com subscribers). True to the admonition Warren wrote in his book that greatness is defined by how much we serve not by how much we receive, and by how much we give away rather than how much we keep, the Warrens announced that they would pay back the compensation they had received from Saddleback Community Church over the years and begin reverse tithing. In other words, they would give away 90 percent of the royalties and keep a mere 10 percent. That connected with people too.

With all of Saddleback Community Church's success you might wonder what's next. Now Rick Warren and the Saddleback Community Church have set their sights on creating a global movement that mobilizes churches worldwide to feed the poor, heal the sick, and help the hopeless, a mission infused with human value.[1] With his connection-oriented leadership style, I expect we're just beginning to see the impact Pastor Rick and his network of pastors will have on the world.

Application

Rick Warren increased inspiring identity and human value by teaching values such as "love your neighbor" that resonated with Saddleback Community Church members. He increased human value by mobilizing the church members to take care of fellow small group members and to reach out to the poor. Knowledge flow increased at Saddleback Community Church by teaching people to be disciplined about listening to one another. What do you do on a day-to-day basis that allows you to intentionally connect with others? Are you aware of your connection with other people in all aspects of your life? What small steps could you take that would allow you to connect better with customers?

Day 18: Patriot Playbook

In recent years, the New England Patriots football team has won an astounding three National Football League Championships without a roster of big name stars. A high degree of connection among the team helps explain why the Patriots have been so successful. The beliefs and behaviors of head coach Bill Belichick and quarterback Tom Brady set the tone for the rest of the team and create trust, cooperation, and esprit de corps.

The inspiring identity that Bill Belichick holds out to the team is one of achieving perfection through team effort. Similar to the vision that John Wooden had for his UCLA Bruins basketball team (see Chapter 4), Belichick has his players thinking about how to improve themselves and their teammates in order to make the Patriots the best they can possibly become. He doesn't rely on emotionalism or stirring up hate against the opposing team. Instead, he focuses on statistics such as fumbles, interceptions, sacks, pass completion percentages, and other forms of objective, unambiguous performance measurement. Continuous improvement to reach perfection is Belichick's and his players' relentless goal.

To increase connection among the players, Belichick doesn't single out players for punishment. He makes the whole team do more work when a single player commits an error, which encourages players to help one another.

Belichick emphasizes one intangible factor: his players' selflessness for the sake of the team. He shows no reluctance to bench egotistical players who act selfish. Belichick has also been willing to trade a talented player whose salary demands work against team connection.

Quarterback Tom Brady epitomizes the kind of team player that Belichick admires. Players around the league admire Brady for his humility and commitment to his teammates. An enthusiastic Dallas Cowboys receiver, Keyshawn Johnson, gushed that "the guy just turned twenty-eight . . . three Super Bowls at that age . . . Un-freakin'-believable. And with his attitude, he's not done. I bet he's got three more in him."

Many of Brady's attributes increase human value in the Patriots culture. In early 2005, Brady stunned sportswriters by accepting a six-year, $60 million contract that was $38 million below the contract of Indianapolis Colts star quarterback Peyton Manning. Brady explained that he wanted the team to have the money available for other players. *Sports Illustrated* senior writer Peter King wrote that in covering football for sixteen years he had never seen anything like that, and "if you think that plays well in the locker room, you're right." *Sports Illustrated* named Brady its 2005 Sportsman of the Year and noted that Brady's "greatest achievement grows out of a generosity of spirit." When MasterCard wanted Brady to pitch its product in a major television advertisement, Brady insisted that his offensive linemen join him in the ad, or he would have to pass.

Belichick increased human value on the team by giving his assistant coaches considerable autonomy in making decisions, and he increased knowledge flow by communicating with players in the weekly team captains' meeting. This marked a considerable change from Belichick's time as head coach for the Cleveland Browns when he was criticized for micromanaging and failing to communicate.[1]

With the high level of connection on the New England Patriots team, it will likely be a force in pro football for many years to come.

Application

Bill Belichick increased inspiring identity by holding out to the team a vision of achieving perfection through team effort. His leadership style gave assistant coaches autonomy (human value), and he communicated regularly with players (knowledge flow). Tom Brady increased human value by not demanding the highest possible salary so that more money will be available to keep his teammates with the Patriots. What steps could you take to be more intentional in your leadership style to bring about changes?

DAY 19: HIGH-FIVE MOMENTS

In 1998, with $100,000 of their own money, Richard Tait and Whit Alexander, two former Microsoft employees, decided to create a new board game. Tait came up with the idea when he and his wife were playing games at the home of their friends. The couple easily won Pictionary and were trounced at Scrabble. Pondering how he felt as the winner of one game and loser of another, Tait thought it would be ideal to play a game that involved different skills so that everyone had a chance to shine. That type of game would be more fun, and it would bring people together rather than alienate them in a winner-take-all battle. Tait persuaded Alexander to join him, and together they created the game Cranium.

Cranium became the fastest-selling independent board game in history, selling more than either Pictionary or Trivial Pursuit had in its first year. The company (also named Cranium) went on to shatter industry records by creating games that won the Toy Industry Association's Toy of the Year game award four out of the last five years. It has sold more than 15 million games in ten languages and thirty countries. In 2005, while the toy industry's unit sales were down 6 percent, Cranium's sales were up 50 percent.

To help fund Cranium's growth and increase distribution, Tait and Alexander persuaded CEO Howard Schultz of Starbucks to invest in the new venture and to distribute the game through Starbucks locations. Schultz liked the tie-in with Starbucks's mission to create community. Cranium brought people together, and it increased the connection among them by making everyone feel like a winner.

Tait and Alexander designed the game based on Harvard professor Howard Gardner's theory of multiple intelligences. Gardner has identified at least seven forms of intelligence ranging from musical and linguistic to logical-mathematical. Cranium incorporates challenges that favor each intelligence in hopes that everyone will win part of the game and experience a high-five moment.

Connection is the key to Cranium's success. Take, for example, Cranium's Conga, a game that gets players to learn more about each other, including silly things such as how many marshmallows fit in someone's mouth. One *New York Times* reporter observed, "When Tait describes the Cranium mission, he often sounds less like a game maker and more like a sociologist diagnosing the ills of an atomized society." *Inc.* magazine opined that "in their minds they weren't selling a game but a social experience." In the words of Tait, "we [want] everyone to high-five their teammate at least once each game . . . I know that's not a very scientific metric, but that's what we're going for." Alexander adds, "We want people to leave a game feeling enriched and better-connected."

Cranium is just as passionate and intentional about increasing connection among its employees. Cranium's inspiring identity is to bring people together in a world that has less free time and more distractions that inhibit connection. Another aspect of Cranium's inspiring identity is that the company gives back to the community, frequently donating games to people in need. In addition, every employee gets ten games to give away to family members and five to donate to charities. Cranium employees are proud of their company, not only for its reputation as an innovator but also for its worthwhile mission and its heart.

Always the passionate leader, Tait reads two hundred customer e-mails and letters on an average day and shares some of them with employees. Celeste Welch wrote about the fun her family has had playing Cranium's games after her two-year-old daughter, Valerie, was diagnosed in 2005 with a brain tumor. Even during the difficult times, Cranium's games Cariboo, Hullabaloo, and Balloon Lagoon kept Valerie, her parents, and her three sisters laughing and smiling. According to Celeste, "[Our kids] never really went through a time of crying or confusion. Really, it's our faith in God that's getting us through. But the Cranium games kept that laughter in the house."

Human value is present in Cranium's workplace culture. New employees go through an orientation program to learn more about Cranium's values, including its goal to produce every Cranium toy or game to meet the CHIFF standard (that means it is clever, high quality, innovative, friendly, and fun). The company throws a Gong Party for new employees. The company pays 100 percent of employee health, dental, and vision care premiums. All of the corner offices with nice views are unoccupied so that everyone can enjoy them. Each employee chooses his or her own title. Tait's title is Grand Poo Bah, and Alexander's is Chief Noodler. Other fun titles include Edgar Allen P. O. (the head of purchasing) and Head of the Hive (the head of public relations who creates buzz about Cranium's products).

In a culture such as Cranium's, knowledge flow is high. The approachable and unpretentious Tait and Alexander exemplify leaders who are more interested in "getting it right" than personally "being right." The collaboration and informality they encourage make people more likely to share their knowledge with decision makers.

The high degree of connection that is fostered by Cranium products and in Cranium's workplace culture contributes to its superior performance and industry leadership. "What Cranium did was it rewrote the rules," says toy industry analyst Chris Byrne. "There's a warmth . . . from the interpersonal interaction that comes from Cranium. People are hungry for that kind of connectedness." I couldn't agree more.[1]

Application

In the words of Cranium co-founder and Chief Noodler Whit Alexander, "we want people to leave a game feeling enriched and better-connected." Would you be inspired to work for a company that aspires to bring people together? Does your organization have an inspiring mission or values? Are your colleagues proud to work for your company? If they are, why? If not, is there some aspect of the company they should be proud of? Could your company help improve connection in the world?

Day 20: Transforming the Culture of Kim

Nestlé Waters North America sells fifteen brands of water, including Arrowhead, Ozarka, Poland Spring, Perrier, and Pellegrino. It has 7,500 employees. Like many companies, it has experienced a number of mergers and acquisitions that combined organizations with different cultures. In 1992, Kim Jeffery was appointed president of Nestlé Waters North America. His challenge was to create a cohesive culture where everyone felt like a member of the same team. This was no small challenge given that the culture Jeffery inherited had been described as "every man for himself."

In 1994, Jeffery received a wake-up call from a 360-degree performance review. While he viewed himself as an engaging leader who inspired people, the review made it clear that people thought of him as abrupt and unapproachable. Many feared him.

Kim believed that putting people in jobs they liked, where they worked alongside people they liked, would bring out the best in them. He also knew that creating the right culture at Nestlé Waters was necessary for the organization to prosper. Furthermore, when the day came for him to leave the firm, he wanted to be sure that a positive culture would be his legacy.

The performance review let Jeffery know that the reality of his leadership style didn't live up to what he desired. He was effectively committing self-sabotage. Now that he understood the situation, he committed himself to fix it. Through ongoing constructive feedback and executive coaching, Jeffery changed. His change, in turn, became the catalyst to increase connection.

The inspiring identity that motivates people at Nestlé Waters North America is the organization's culture, especially that it is a place where people are truly valued. Kim's actions reinforce this message. On one occasion, he learned that Jorge Crespo, a limo driver who regularly drove the firm's employees, had a daughter who was diagnosed with meningitis and that Jorge didn't have insurance to cover the medical costs to treat her. Jeffery wrote a blank check, gave it to Jorge, and told him to "take care of your daughter and fill in the amount afterward."

On his way to interview with Nestlé Waters in 1997, Dimitrios Smyrnios learned from Jorge how Jeffery helped him pay for his daughter's medical treatments. Hearing the story gave Smyrnios a favorable impression of the company and its president. He subsequently joined the firm and is currently vice president of the home and office division. In 1999, Smyrnios followed Kim's example. He demonstrated how much the Nestlé Waters' culture values people when he approved substantial bonuses to employees in the Florida division despite the division's underperformance after Hurricane George hit the state. The generous bonuses were paid to thank those employees for their tireless efforts to provide bottled water to hurricane victims.

Employees are proud of the organization's active involvement in local community programs such as Kids in Crisis and the Boys and Girls Club. The firm provides both financial support and volunteers. Jeffery and his wife led a fund-raising campaign that raised $7.5 million for Kids in Crisis.

Nestlé Waters North America benefits from human value because it has an informal, friendly culture in which colleagues focus their competitive energy on external competitors rather than on one another. Human value is increased by Kim's belief in work/life balance. When he isn't traveling, Jeffery is usually in the office by 8:30 a.m. and home by 6:00 p.m.

Potential new employees are carefully screened to ensure they share the company's values. Every potential new hire has to spend an eight-hour-day riding with a water route delivery person during which the candidate is closely scrutinized. Only candidates who treat everyone with respect, regardless of rank, make the cut at Nestlé Waters. The firm's culture is reinforced through training programs that clarify values and emphasize the personal stories of participants to help them see where the values apply in their day-to-day work.

Knowledge flow is present in the firm's culture because of the open-door, informal environment and embrace of communication outside the chain of command. The firm's training programs increase knowledge flow by bringing people together from various parts of the organization.

Despite aggressive moves into the water market by Pepsi and Coca-Cola, Nestlé Waters North America continues to lead the industry with reported revenues of $2.74 billion and 27.9 percent market share in 2004, the latest year reported. Jeffery and Nestlé Waters North America have come a long way since the 1994 performance review that set him in motion to improve his organization's culture. In a recent article Jeffery identified connection as one reason for his organization's success when he said, "Having a great culture is a competitive advantage because we have people pulling all the oars together and a common mission."[1]

Application

Jeffery increased inspiring identity by making Nestlé Waters North America a company with a reputation for a caring culture. He increased human value by scrutinizing potential employees to be certain they showed respect to all people regardless of their rank in the organization. He increased knowledge flow by embracing communication outside the chain of command. If you had a 360-degree performance review today, what do you think it would communicate? Would it show that you care about your colleagues and that you build inspiring identity, human value, and knowledge flow within your organization? Would you be willing to make the kinds of changes Kim Jeffery made?

CONCLUSION

BUILD A FIRE THAT LASTS

A strong sense of connection among people in an organization fires them up and improves both individual and organizational performance. The lack of connection will gradually burn them out. Research—by sociologists, psychologists, and neuroscientists—and anecdotal evidence point to these conclusions. So does research by well-respected companies such as Gallup and the Corporate Executive Board that measures engagement and connection in organizations. The stories of leaders of businesses, nations, sports teams, and social sector organizations illustrate that connection boosts performance.

Inspiring identity, human value, and knowledge flow are the elements in a culture to increase connection and help people and organizations thrive. These elements meet deeply rooted human needs for respect, recognition, belonging, autonomy, personal growth, and meaning. The elements in a culture that create connection are present when people exhibit the universal character strengths celebrated by moral philosophers and religious leaders over the ages.

The historian David McCullough was right when he observed:

> While there are indeed great, often unfathomable forces in history before which even the most exceptional of individuals seem insignificant, the wonder is how often events turn upon a single personality, or the quality we call character.[1]

The legendary UCLA basketball coach John Wooden made a keen observation when he stated one of his favorite maxims: "ability may get you to the top, but only character will keep you there."[2] The Reverend Martin Luther King Jr. stated in his "I Have a Dream" speech, "I have a dream that my four little children will one day live in a nation where they will not be judged by the color of their skin but by the content of their character."

Indeed, character development and connection among the people of the world are critical to our future. So much is at risk if we ignore them.

The need to increase connection and strengthen character in the business world could not be greater, given the fact that a mere quarter of Americans feel connected and engaged at work, we face an impending labor shortage in some sectors, and the ongoing globalization of labor threatens the loss of jobs overseas in others. The benefits of increased productivity and innovation await those organizations that unleash the power of connection. A connection culture is truly a win-win outcome for organizations and the individuals who inhabit them.

What Legacy Will You Leave?

All of us, at some point in our lives, wonder how we will be remembered. What legacy will we leave? An outstanding example of an intentional connector I presented earlier was John Wooden.

Coach Wooden's legacy and his connection with his players become clear when you consider Bill Walton's reflections written in 2000 about the impact that Wooden had and still has on Walton's life:

> [Coach Wooden] taught us life at UCLA . . . I call him on the phone constantly and go see him as often as possible . . . I always sit . . . as close as physically possible to this remarkable spirit . . . at 89 . . . he is still the same teacher, the same positive force, the same person we would like to become, only better . . . I've taken my kids to his house, the same house he lived in since 1973 . . . his former players . . . always ask him to let us put a financial package together for him so he can buy his mansion on a hill . . . but every time he tells us no. The joy and happiness in John Wooden's life comes today, as it always has, from the success of others. He regularly tells us what he learned from his two favorite teachers, Abraham Lincoln and Mother Teresa, is that a life not lived for others is a life not lived . . . I thank John Wooden every day for his selfless gifts, his lessons, his time, his vision, and especially his patience. This is why we call him coach.[3]

Who wouldn't want to have a legacy like that! In an interview a few years ago, Wooden expressed that although he appreciates the many trophies, awards, and honors he received over his long and successful career, the trophies he is most proud of are the men that his former players became.[4] In other words, the character strengths that Wooden sees today in the men he helped shape are his legacy and a source of joy to him.

How will your friends and family remember you? How about your colleagues? If you are a highly visible leader, how will history remember you? It's important to consider your legacy early in life when there is sufficient time to be intentional about living in a way that's consistent with how you want to be remembered. As Jason Pankau likes to say, "Live with the end in mind." A life coach for executives, he frequently finds that many of the people he coaches reach the latter years of their careers before they realize they didn't live with the end in mind. Then they typically try to repair the damage done from their earlier actions.

How about you? Will you be remembered as an intentional connector such as John Wooden, George Washington, or Frances Hesselbein, or will you be remembered as an intentional or unintentional disconnector such as Howell Raines, Al Dunlap, or Frederick the Great during the latter years of his reign?

Evidence suggests that leaders of enduring organizations take their legacies seriously. In 1983 Royal Dutch/Shell Group studied twenty-seven companies that had survived more than one hundred years, were still important in their industries, and continued to have strong corporate identities. One finding was that managers of these organizations believed it was important to leave their organizations in as good as or better shape than when they became managers. These managers also put a higher priority on people than on assets. Keeping the team together was more significant to them than the type of work they did. In fact, each of the twenty-seven companies had changed its business portfolio at least once. For example, the chemical company DuPont began as a gunpowder company, and Mitsui of Japan began as a drapery shop before it moved successively into banking, mining, and manufacturing.[5] Effectively, these managers thought of themselves as trustees or stewards, who had a responsibility to the current and future members of their work communities. Wise leaders appreciate the contributions of the people in their organizations and therefore have a sense of stewardship toward those people.

The root cause of leaders who leave less desirable legacies can often be traced to a failure of character. Bill Thrall, Bruce McNichol, and Ken McElrath in their book, *The Ascent of a Leader,* describe the pattern of leaders who advance in responsibility without having developed sufficient character strengths to prepare for leadership.

> Many men and women of influence discover that leadership is like a ladder—a challenging and unpredictable climb, often stable at the bottom and unpredictable and shaky at the top. From the bottom, life at the top looks appealing, even alluring, and many leaders attack the ladder with gusto, confident that they possess what it takes to conquer the rungs.
>
> Yet, when these leaders reach positions of authority, unforeseen instability begins to surface. Such issues as the pressure of success, the temptation of privilege, the demands of followers, and the isolation of leadership leave deep depressions on the rungs—caused by the white-knuckle grip of the leader. Many look for a way to stabilize their situation, but too many leaders come crashing down. And when they land, few are there to help. Some will even laugh.[6]

According to one extensive study, more than 70 percent of leaders do not finish well.[7] This should not be a surprise. Absent strength of character and the self-knowledge that comes from staying connected with others, leaders set themselves up for failure.

Connection and character protect leaders from falling into the traps of leadership failure. Manfred F. R. Kets de Vries, the director of Insead's Global Leadership Center, professor of leadership development, and practicing psychoanalyst, has devoted his life to studying CEOs. Kets de Vries has noted that too many leaders lead lives of chronic imbalance and delude themselves into believing they don't. Habitual imbalance in a leader's life not only hurts the leader but also hurts his family and the organization he leads. The leader often surrounds himself with yes-men and becomes blinded by narcissism. These patterns lead to excessive risk taking to ease the feelings of guilt, boredom, and depression that stalk him. Kets de Vries describes a healthy leader as someone who, among other things, has "the capacity to establish and maintain healthy relationships" (in other words, a healthy leader is an intentional connector).[8]

The person who becomes relationally isolated and thus lacks connection with others during his work career will have few family members and friends who will want to spend time with him later in life. The failure to connect with family and friends will eventually calcify, making it nearly impossible to establish later on. The absence of connection is taken as rejection, and bitterness can become permanently attached to the broken relationship. Too many people succumb to this fate that could have been avoided.

It Begins with You

In the end, you are the key to increasing connection and avoiding the fate of those who fail to connect with others. A connection culture is constructed one person at a time. Each of us has the responsibility to grow in character and become an intentional connector. This applies especially to leaders because they are in a position to be people developers and others may emulate them. Organizations blessed with such leaders have many other people in the organization who are intentional connectors too.

My hope is that this book has made a modest contribution to persuading you and encouraging you to be intentional about increasing connection and developing character strengths. May the words of Edmund Burke, the British statesman and humanitarian, encourage each of us in that endeavor: "the only thing necessary for the triumph of evil is for good men to do nothing."[9]

Burke's comments apply to the evils in society as well as the evil within ourselves. To bring out the best in yourself and others, I encourage you to put into practice the suggestions offered throughout this book and to share this book with others who would benefit from its message.

With that, I want to wish you the very best of connections with your family members, your friends and neighbors, your colleagues at work, and your fellow members in society. And may the strength of these connections bless you and help you maintain the fire of inspiration, energy, and enthusiasm all of the days of your life.

Review, Reflection, and Application

- ☐ Good character increases connection, which in turn improves individual and organizational performance.

- ☐ The character of individuals often changes history, and sustainable superior performance isn't achievable without good character.

- ☐ With low employee engagement and the coming labor shortage, the time is now to improve the character strengths of people in organizations and the connection among them.

- ☐ Because few people are intentional about developing character strengths, most fail to leave a legacy of which they can be genuinely proud. John Wooden is an excellent model to follow. He developed his character and the character of his basketball players, many of whom have written in books and articles about Wooden's positive impact on them as people.

- ☐ What do you want your legacy to be with your family and friends, your coworkers, and the people in your community? Are you on course to achieve the legacy you desire? If not, what must you do to get on course?

- ☐ So what? Increasing connection in a culture happens one person at a time. Just as developing character strengths and connection requires us to be intentional, developing the legacy we desire requires intentionality. Will you be intentional, or will you just drift through life? Remember that when we drift, it is always toward character weakness. Each of us needs to improve our character and encourage others to do the same. Our future depends on it.

APPENDIX A

Questions to Assess Organizational Culture and Connection

Do your closest coworkers know you as a person, including your life outside work, what's important to you, and what talents and skills you possess?

Do your closest coworkers care about you as a person, including what's happening in your life outside work?

Do your closest coworkers know the major events in your life that shaped your beliefs and who you have become?

Do you know the major events in the lives of your closest coworkers and how they shaped their beliefs and who they have become?

What kind of activities could be planned for your team to facilitate getting to know one another better?

Do your closest coworkers appreciate your strengths?

Do your closest coworkers share their personal trials and triumphs and support one another?

Do you receive praise and recognition for your work? How?

Do you have someone at work who is a mentor to you and who wants to help you grow? If not, who would you like to have as a mentor and why?

Do you feel your supervisor makes certain that you have work that appropriately challenges your skills? Explain.

What type of training do you receive to help you develop professionally?

Are you continuously learning and growing at work?

Would you classify your closest coworkers as trusted colleagues or competitors? What makes you feel one way or the other?

Do people at work feel it's safe to be who they really are, or do they put on an act to fit in?

How is your compensation determined, and do you feel the process is fair?

Do you understand how your job performance is assessed, and do you feel the process is fair?

How often do you receive performance reviews? Are they given with sufficient regularity and with sufficient substance and clarity to help you grow?

Are you treated fairly in the areas of compensation, promotions, job assignments, or other aspects of your job? Explain.

Is your supervisor open with you so that you know what he or she thinks and believes about work issues that affect you? If you have asked for more information, how was that request treated?

Does your supervisor consistently seek your opinions, listen to you, and carefully consider your views before making decisions on important issues that affect you and your work? Do your coworkers?

Do you consistently seek your coworkers' opinions, listen to them, and carefully consider their views before making decisions on important issues that affect them and their work?

Are you encouraged to think of ways to improve your organization?

Are you encouraged to stay informed about developments outside your work environment that affect your organization (for example, developments in your industry and among your competitors)? What might you do to keep "your eyes and ears open"?

What is the process at work to systematically keep people informed and provide them an open, honest, and safe forum to share their views?

How has your organization's history and important events and stories shaped what it has become today?

Is there a group that gets together to talk about a vision for the future as it relates to your work? Does the group include members from across the organization?

APPENDIX A

Have you been a part of a discussion about shared beliefs as they relate to your workplace (for example, obeying the law, being honest in communications, helping one another, promptly returning colleagues' phone calls, etc.)?

Do you and your colleagues share a sense of importance about the work done by your organization?

Do you feel your work is important? Why?

Are your colleagues proud of your organization, its reputation, its work, and its accomplishments? Why?

Do your colleagues have high standards of excellence for their work?

Are some people considered to be and treated like stars and others thought of and treated like second-class citizens? Explain your answer.

Do any of your coworkers ever make you feel inferior to them? If so, how?

Do you understand how decisions are made, and do you feel they are fair? Explain your answer.

What other aspects are right, wrong, or missing in your environment at work?

How do you feel about your future in your organization?

Based on your answers to these questions, where do you see areas that require improvement?

NOTES

Although I have not counted them, the interviews, books, articles, and speeches I consulted while doing research for this book had to number well over one thousand. Throughout the book I added notes to give credit to individuals whose ideas influenced me and where I thought readers might be interested in following up on some of my source material. I did not note sources where I believed the information was, for the most part, common knowledge to the average reader of books and periodicals about management and leadership or readily available in reference materials such as encyclopedias. If there are any inadvertent errors or misinterpretations of the materials consulted, the sole responsibility is mine.

—Michael Lee Stallard

Introduction

1. Based on surveys of more than one million employees, Gallup research has reported employee engagement in America has fluctuated between 25 percent and 29 percent since 2000. See James K. Clifton, "Engaging Your Employees: Six Keys to Understanding the New Workplace," http://shrm.org/foundation/engaging.asp, and John H. Fleming, Curt Coffman, and James K. Harter, "Manage Your Human Sigma," *Harvard Business Review* (July-August 2005): 107–14. I chose to present the 25 percent figure in light of other research (see note 5 below) that indicates employee engagement may be even lower. Whatever the case, the point here is that the overwhelming majority of workers are disengaged.
2. David G. Myers, *American Paradox: Spiritual Hunger in an Age of Plenty* (New Haven: Yale University Press, 2001).
3. Robert E. Lane, *The Loss of Happiness in Market Democracies* (New Haven: Yale University Press, 2000).
4. David Brooks, "One Nation, Slightly Divisible," *Atlantic Online*, December 2001, http://www.theatlantic.com/issues/2001/12/brooks.htm.
5. Corporate Leadership Council, "Driving Performance and Retention Through Employee Engagement" (Washington, D.C.: Corporate Executive Board, 2004). An executive summary of the reports is available at http://www.corporateleadershipcouncil.com/CLC/1,1283,00Public_Display115952,00.html.
6. Several books have influenced my thinking on the different personality types and the right brain-directed powers of intuition, including the following: Daniel H. Pink, *A Whole New Mind: Why Right-Brainers Will Rule the Future* (New York: Penguin, 2005); David G. Myers, *Intuition: Its Powers and Perils* (New Haven: Yale University Press, 2002); Malcolm Gladwell, *Blink: The Power of Thinking Without Thinking* (New York: Little, Brown, 2005); David Keirsey, *Please Understand Me II: Temperament, Character, Intelligence* (Del Mar: Prometheus Nemesis Book Company, 1998).

NOTES

7. Otto Kroeger with Janet M. Thuesen, *Type Talk at Work: How the 16 Personality Types Determine Your Success on the Job* (New York: Delacorte Press, 1992), 391–98.
8. Betsy Morris, "The Best Place to Work Now," *Fortune,* 11 January 2006, 79–84.
9. Regina Fazio Maruca, ed., *What Managers Say, What Employees Hear: Connecting with Your Front Line (So They'll Connect with Customers)* (Westport: Praeger, 2006), 131–32.
10. William C. Taylor and Polly LaBarre, "How Pixar Adds a New School of Thought to Disney," *New York Times,* 29 January 2006, section 3, p. 3.
11. Except where noted, my basis for making the statements in this section comes from various conversations with individuals who work at these organizations or who closely monitor their activities.

Chapter 1: The Case for Connection at Work

1. See James K. Harter, Frank L. Schmidt, and Theodore L. Hayes, "Business-Unit-Level Relationship Between Employee Satisfaction, Employee Engagement, and Business Outcomes: A Meta-Analysis," *Journal of Applied Psychology* 87, no. 2 (2002): 268–79. I will explain in subsequent paragraphs why I believe this study based on Gallup's Q12 questionnaire is an excellent indicator of connection.
2. Ibid. The Gallup study performed a meta-analysis on data from surveys conducted between 1992 and 1999. The surveys collectively included 198,524 respondents in 7,939 business units of 36 companies. Gallup used its 12 question Gallup Workplace Audit that measures employee engagement and compared it to several business outcomes (i.e., customer satisfaction, productivity, profit, employee turnover, and accidents). The study concluded that the correlation between employee engagement and business outcomes was substantial (corrected for independent variable measurement error yielded a correlation of .38 between employee engagement and the set of business outcomes measured). Also note that a subsequent study identified the relationship between employee engagement and business outcomes goes both ways (i.e., higher business outcomes produce a higher level of employee engagement), and that the relationship effect of positive business outcomes on employee engagement exceeded the effect of employee engagement on business outcomes. This doesn't surprise me because there is a mutual relationship between employee engagement and performance. See Benjamin Schneider, Paul J. Hanges, D. Brent Smith, and Amy Nichole Salvaggio, "Which Comes First: Employee Attitudes or Organizational Financial and Market Performance?" *Journal of Applied Psychology* 88, no. 5 (2003): 836–51.
3. Corporate Leadership Council, "Driving Performance and Retention Through Employee Engagement."
4. Hewitt Associates LLC, "The Link Between Employee Retention and Business Results," *Hewitt Magazine,* http://was4.hewitt.com/hewitt/resource/rptspubs/hewitt_magazine/vol16_iss2/features/ezine.html.
5. Based on surveys of more than one million employees, Gallup research has reported employee engagement in America has fluctuated between 25 percent and 29 percent. See Clifton, "Engaging Your Employees: Six Keys to Understanding the New Workplace," and Fleming, Coffman, and Harter, "Manage Your Human Sigma."

6. Corporate Leadership Council, "Driving Performance and Retention Through Employee Engagement."
7. Tom Rath and Donald O. Clifton, *How Full Is Your Bucket?: Positive Strategies for Work and Life* (New York: Gallup Press, 2004), 33.
8. Phillip Longman, "The Global Baby Bust," *Foreign Affairs* (May-June 2004): 64–79.
9. Ken Dychtwald, Tamara Erickson, and Bob Morison, "It's Time to Retire Retirement," *Harvard Business Review* (March 2004): 49–57.
10. *The American Workplace: Building America's Workforce for the 21st Century* (Washington, D.C.: Employment Policy Foundation, 2001).
11. Dychtwald, Erickson, and Morison, "It's Time to Retire Retirement."
12. Sydney Finkelstein, *Why Smart Executives Fail: And What You Can Learn from Their Mistakes* (New York: Portfolio, 2003).

Chapter 2: The Science of Connection

1. Edward M. Hallowell, MD, "The Human Moment at Work," *Harvard Business Review* (January-February 1999): 58–66. Also see Edward M. Hallowell, MD, *Connect: 12 Vital Ties That Open Your Heart, Lengthen Your Life, and Deepen Your Soul* (New York: Pantheon, 1999).
2. Joyce K. Fletcher, Judith V. Gordon, and Jean Baker Miller, "Women and the Workplace: Applications of a Psychodynamic Theory," *American Journal of Psychoanalysis* 60, no. 3 (2000). Also see the Jean Baker Miller Training Institute Web site at http://www.wellesley.edu/JBMTI.
3. Most of the physiological effects of connection were sourced from Edward Hallowell's excellent book, *Connect: 12 Vital Ties That Open Your Heart, Lengthen Your Life, and Deepen Your Soul*, 5–9. For more recent evidence on the impact of connection with infants see William J. Cromie, "Of Hugs and Hormones," *Harvard University Gazette*, 11 June 1998, http://www.news.harvard.edu/gazette/1998/06.11/OfHugsandHormon.html.
4. Connection brings about positive emotions that have been determined to improve decision making and creativity; see Barbara L. Frederickson, "The Value of Positive Emotions," *American Scientist* 91 (July-August 2003): 330–35.
5. An excellent review of the research on the factors that contribute to subjective well-being can be found at Richard M. Ryan and Edward L. Deci, "On Happiness and Human Potentials: A Review of Research on Hedonic and Eudaimonic Well-Being," ed. S. Fiske, *Annual Review of Psychology* 52 (Palo Alto: Annual Reviews, Inc., 2001): 141–66. This article can be accessed at http://www.psych.rochester.edu/SDT/documents/2001RyanDeci_AnnRev.pdf.
6. A. H. Maslow, "A Theory of Human Motivation," *Psychological Review* 50 (1943): 370–96.
7. Ibid.

Chapter 3: The Connection Culture

1. Alan Deutschman, *The Second Coming of Steve Jobs* (New York: Broadway Books, 2000), 251–53; Stuart Elliott, "Apple Endorses Some Achievers Who 'Think Different,'" *New York Times*, 3 August 1998.

2. Doris Kearns Goodwin, *No Ordinary Time: Franklin and Eleanor Roosevelt: The Home Front in World War II* (New York: Simon & Schuster, 1994), 340; *Encarta Encyclopedia Online,* s.v. "Aircraft Production During World War II," http://encarta.msn.com/media_701500594_761563737_1_1/Aircraft_Production_During_World_War_II.html.
3. Barbara S. Peterson, *Blue Streak: Inside jetBlue, the Upstart That Rocked an Industry* (New York: Simon & Schuster, 1994), xiv.
4. Jack Mitchell, *Hug Your Customers: The Proven Way to Personalize Sales and Achieve Astounding Results* (New York: Hyperion, 2003), 145–46.
5. Brian Hanessian and Carlos Sierra, "Leading a Turnaround: An Interview with the Chairman of D&B," *McKinsey Quarterly,* no. 2 (2005).
6. Joseph Stallard (head of recruiting and training, Sewell Automotive Corporation), discussion with the author, December 2005.
7. Beth Belton, "Procter & Gamble's Renovator-in-Chief," *Business Week Online,* 11 December 2002, www.busnessweek.com/bwdaily/dnflash/dec2002/nf20021211_7599.htm; Robert Berner, "A Catalyst and Encourager of Change," *Business Week Online,* 7 July 2003, http://businessweek.com/print/magazine/content/03_27/b3840014_mz001.htm; Katrina Booker, "The Un-CEO," *Fortune,* 16 September 2002, 88–96; Cliff Peale, "The Lafley Method: Face the Facts, Think Like a Customer," *Cincinnati Enquirer Online,* 9 June 2002, http://www.enquirer.com/editions/2002/06/09/fin_the_lafley_method.html; James R. Stengel, Andrea L. Dixon, and Chris T. Allen, "Listening Begins at Home," *Harvard Business Review* (November 2003): 106–16.

Chapter 4: Connection and the Legend

1. Except where noted, the material in this chapter was sourced from John Wooden and Steve Jamison, *My Personal Best: Life Lessons from an All-American Journey* (New York: McGraw-Hill, 2004).
2. Tracy Pierson, "UCLA to Honor John Wooden," 19 December 2003, http://www.medaloffreedom.com/JohnRWoodenUCLAFloor.htm.
3. Bill Walton, "John Wooden, Like UCLA, Simply the Best," http://www.billwalton.com/wooden.html.
4. Ibid.
5. Kareem Abdul-Jabbar, "Appreciating the Wisdom of Wooden: As a Coach, Brilliant. As a Man, He Means So Much More," *New York Times,* 10 December 2000.
6. Walton, "John Wooden, Like UCLA, Simply the Best."
7. Ibid.
8. Ibid.

Chapter 5: Trouble in Times Square

1. The material from this chapter was sourced from Ken Auletta, "The Howell Doctrine," *New Yorker,* 26 July 2004; and Matthew Rose and Laurie P. Cohen, "Amid Turmoil, Top Editors Resign at New York Times," *Wall Street Journal,* 6 June 2003.

NOTES

Chapter 6: The Next Step in the Evolution of Organizations

1. Thanks to Mitchell Dickey for sharing his thoughts and white papers on his Tasks + Relationships = Results model with me that helped shape my thoughts about the problem of employee disengagement and disconnection.
2. For additional thoughts on star systems see Malcolm Gladwell, "The Talent Myth: Are Smart People Overrated?" *New Yorker*, 22 July 2002.
3. Thomas DeLong and Vineeta Vijayaraghavan, "Let's Hear It for B Players," *Harvard Business Review* (June 2003): 96–102.
4. Jon R. Katzenbach and Jason A. Santamaria, "Firing Up the Front Line," *Harvard Business Review* (May 1999): 107–17.

Chapter 7: Inspire with Identity

1. Facts about the Manhattan Project were sourced from Warren Bennis and Patricia A. Biederman. *Organizing Genius* (Reading: Addison-Wesley, 1997), 204–5; Don E. Beyer, *The Manhattan Project: America Makes the First Atomic Bomb* (New York: Franklin Watts, 1991).
2. Richard Feynman, "Los Alamos from Below: Reminiscences 1943–1945," http://calteches.library.caltech.edu/14/01/FeynmanLosAlamos.pdf.
3. Simon Schama, *A History of Britain: At the Edge of the World, 3500 B.C.–1603 A.D.* (New York: Hyperion, 2000), 266.
4. The Literature Network, King Henry V, Act 4. Scene III, http://www.online-literature.com/view.php/henryV/21?term=band%20of%20brothers.
5. Viktor E. Frankl, *Man's Search for Meaning: An Introduction to Logotherapy* (New York: Simon & Schuster, 1984), 82–88.

Chapter 8: Create Meaning in Your Organization

1. Keith H. Hammonds, "Michael Porter's Big Ideas," *Fast Company*, February 2001.
2. David Brooks, *On Paradise Drive: How We Live Now (and Always Have) in the Future Tense* (New York: Simon & Schuster, 2004), 220–21.
3. United States Marine Corps, History Division, *Who's Who in Marine Corps History*, "Sergeant Major Daniel 'Dan' Joseph Daly, USMC (Deceased)," http://hqinet001.hqmc.usmc.mil/HD/Historical/Whos_Who/Daly_DJ.htm.

Chapter 9: Delete What Devalues

1. Bernard Bailyn, *Ideological Origins of the American Revolution* (Boston: Harvard University Press, 1967), 202–4; Barbara W. Tuchman, *The March of Folly: From Troy to Vietnam* (New York: Alfred A. Knopf, 1984), 128–231.
2. Gordon S. Wood, *The Radicalism of the American Revolution* (New York: Alfred A. Knopf, 1992), 6–7.
3. Brooks, *On Paradise Drive: How We Live Now (and Always Have) in the Future Tense*, 80–81.
4. Lilia M. Cortina, Vicki J. Magley, Jill Hunter-Williams, and Regina Day Langhout, "Incivility in the Workplace: Incidence and Impact," *Journal of Occupational Health Psychology* 6 (2001): 64–80.
5. Jerry Useem, "A Manager for All Seasons," *Fortune*, 30 April 2001.

6. James MacGregor Burns, *Transforming Leadership* (New York: Atlantic Monthly Press, 2003), 110–12.
7. Isser Woloch, *The New Regime: Transformations of the French Civic Order, 1789–1820s* (New York: W. W. Norton, 1994), 432–33.
8. Louis Menand, *The Metaphysical Club: A Story of Ideas in America* (New York: Farrar, Straus and Giroux, 2001), 289–306.
9. Based on author's conversations with various officials at Goodyear.

Chapter 10: Dial Up the Value

1. Mihaly Csikszentmihalyi, *Flow: The Psychology of Optimal Experience* (New York: Harper & Row, 1990).
2. For the story of how Taiichi Ohno developed Lean Manufacturing (also called the Toyota Production System), see Maryann Keller, *Collision: GM, Toyota, Volkswagen and the Race to Own the 21st Century* (New York: Doubleday, 1993), 154–93.
3. Doris Kearns Goodwin, "Lessons of Presidential Leadership," *Leader to Leader* 9 (summer 1998): 23–30.

Chapter 11: Three Benefits of Knowledge Flow

1. Belton, "Procter & Gamble's Renovator-in-Chief"; Berner, "A Catalyst and Encourager of Change"; Booker, "The Un-CEO"; Peale, "The Lafley Method: Face the Facts, Think Like a Customer"; Stengel, Dixon, and Allen, "Listening Begins at Home".
2. Burns, *Transforming Leadership*, 105–8.
3. Roger Mudd, *American Heritage: Great Minds of History* (New York: John Wiley & Sons, 1999), 185–96.
4. Andrew S. Grove, *Swimming Across* (New York: Warner Books, 2002).
5. Andrew S. Grove, *Only the Paranoid Survive: How to Exploit the Crisis Points That Challenge Every Company and Career* (New York: Doubleday, 1996); Richard N. Langlois and W. Edward Steinmueller, "Strategy and Circumstance: The Response of American Firms to Japanese Competition in Semiconductors, 1980–1995," *Strategic Management Journal* 21 (2000): 1163–73.
6. zaadz*beta*, Quotes by David Hume, http://www.zaadz.com/quotes/David_Hume ?page=1.
7. *The Debate on the Constitution: Federalist and Antifederalist Speeches, Articles and Letters During the Struggle Over Ratification* (New York: Library Classics of the United States, 1993), 3–5.
8. Ram Charan and Jerry Useem, "Why Companies Fail," *Fortune*, 27 May 2002, 56.
9. Goodwin, "Lessons of Presidential Leadership," 23–30.
10. Tuchman, *The March of Folly: From Troy to Vietnam*, 11–14.
11. Charan and Useem, "Why Companies Fail," 60.
12. Diane Vaughan, *The Challenger Launch Decision: Risky Technology, Culture, and Deviance at NASA* (Chicago: University of Chicago Press, 1996), 394-399.
13. David E. Sanger, "Report of Loss of Shuttle Focuses on NASA Blunders and Issues Somber Warning," *New York Times*, 27 August 2003; William Langewiesche, "Columbia's Last Flight: The Inside Story of the Investigation—and the Catastrophe It Laid Bare," *Atlantic Monthly*, November 2003, 58–87.

14. David Johnston, "The Warnings Were There, But Who Was Listening," *New York Times*, 27 July 2003.
15. Howard Gardner, *Changing Minds: The Art and Science of Changing Our Own and Other People's Minds* (Boston: Harvard Business School Press, 2004), 208; David Rock and Jeffrey Schwartz, "The Neuroscience of Leadership," *Strategy + Business* (summer 2006): 71–80.
16. Michael D. Doubler, *Closing with the Enemy: How GIs Fought the War in Europe, 1944–1945* (Lawrence, KS: University Press of Kansas, 1995), 31–62; Mudd, *American Heritage Great Minds of History*, 195–98. Please note that the sources report different spellings of Curtis Cullen's name and different locations for his hometown (Chicago or New York City).
17. Omar N. Bradley, *A Soldier's Story* (New York: Henry Holt, 1951), 342.
18. Mudd, *American Heritage: Great Minds of History*, 195–98.
19. Based on author's conversations with Starbucks executives.
20. David S. Landis, *The Wealth and Poverty of Nations: Why Some Are So Rich and Some Are So Poor* (New York: W. W. Norton, 1998), 93–98; Dinesh D'Souza, *What's So Great About America* (Washington, D.C.: Regnery, 2002), 50–52.
21. Schneider, Hanges, Smith, and Salvaggio, "Which Comes First: Employee Attitudes or Organizational Financial and Market Performance?" 836–51.

Chapter 12: Increase the Flow

1. The author was formerly an executive of a wholly owned subsidiary of the Charles Schwab Corporation and made these observations during the time of his employment.
2. Ethan M. Rasiel and Paul N. Friga, *The McKinsey Mind* (New York: McGraw-Hill, 2001), 76–79.
3. Ibid.
4. Daniel A. Wren and Ronald G. Greenwood, *Management Innovators: The People and Ideas That Have Shaped Modern Business* (New York: Oxford University Press, 1998), 231.
5. Clayton M. Christensen, *The Innovator's Dilemma: When New Technologies Cause Great Firms to Fail* (Boston: Harvard Business School Press, 1997), xiv.
6. James Montier, "Are Two Heads Better Than One?" Dresdner Wasserstein Securities Limited (2004), quoted in John Mauldin, *Outside the Box* 1, no. 5, 11 October 2004.
7. Richard Dowis, *The Lost Art of the Great Speech: How to Write It, How to Deliver It* (New York: AMA Publications, 2000), 161.
8. For an excellent case in defense of hierarchy see Harold J. Leavitt, *Top Down: Why Hierarchies Are Here to Stay and How to Manage Them More Efficiently* (Boston: Harvard Business School Press, 2004).
9. Joseph Nocera, *A Piece of the Action: How the Middle Class Joined the Money Class* (New York: Simon & Schuster, 1994), 155–60.

Chapter 14: The Journey to Connection

1. Noah Riner, "'06 Welcomes Class of '09," *Dartmouth Review*, 20 September 2005.
2. Reggie Van Lee, Lisa Fabish, and Nancy McGaw, "The Value of Corporate Values," *Strategy + Business* (Summer 2005).

NOTES

Chapter 15: Developing Character Strengths and Connection

1. Public Agenda, 1999, "Kids These Days '99: What Americans Really Think About the Next Generation," 4, (based on Public Agenda's survey of 1,005 adults).
2. William Damon, *Bringing in a New Era in Character Education* (Palo Alto: Hoover Institution Press, 2002), viii.
3. David Rock and Jeffrey Schwartz, "The Neuroscience of Leadership," *Strategy + Business* (Summer 2006): 71–80.
4. Christopher Peterson and Martin E. P. Seligman, *Character Strengths and Virtues: A Handbook and Classification* (Washington, D.C.: American Psychological Association; New York: Oxford University Press, 2004), 51–52; Martin E. P. Seligman and Mihaly Csikszentmihalyi, "Positive Psychology: An Introduction," *American Psychologist* 55 (2000): 5–14.
5. Peterson and Seligman, *Character Strengths and Virtues: A Handbook and Classification*, 28n.
6. Benjamin Franklin, *The Autobiography of Benjamin Franklin* (New York: Random House, 1950).
7. William Lee Miller, *Lincoln's Virtues: An Ethical Biography* (New York: Alfred A. Knopf, 2002).
8. Charles de Montesquieu, *The Spirit of the Laws* (New York: Cambridge University Press, 1989).
9. Carolly Erickson, *The First Elizabeth* (New York: Simon & Schuster, 1983), 171–73, 315.
10. James R. Gaines, *An Evening in the Palace of Reason: Bach Meets Frederick the Great in the Age of Enlightenment* (New York: Fourth Estate, 2005), 248.
11. Steve Reinemund, chairman and CEO, PepsiCo, 7 June 2006 interview by David Miller, Yale Center for Faith and Culture, Greenwich Leadership Forum, Greenwich, CT.
12. Malcolm Gladwell, "The Cellular Church," *New Yorker*, 12 September 2005, 60–67.
13. Christina Hoff Summers, "How Moral Education Is Finding Its Way Back into America's Schools," in *Bringing in a New Era in Character Education*, ed. William Damon (Palo Alto: Hoover Institution Press, 2002), 33.
14. Art Kleiner, "Karen Stephenson's Quantum Theory of Trust," *Strategy + Business*, issue 29 (fourth quarter 2002), 1–14; also see Malcolm Gladwell, "Designs for Working: Why Your Bosses Want to Turn Your New Office into Greenwich Village," *New Yorker*, 11 December 2000, 60–70.

Week 1

Day 1: French Hero of the American Revolution

1. The following sources were used in writing this day's entry: Harlow Giles Unger, *Lafayette* (Hoboken: John Wiley & Sons, 2002); Arthur M. Schlesinger Jr. and John S. Bowman, eds., *The Almanac of American History* (New York: G. P. Putnam's Sons, 1983),126.; Marian Klamkin, *The Return of Lafayette* (New York: Charles Scribner's Sons, 1975), 1–7, 193.

Day 2: Restoring the Glory

1. The following sources were used in writing this day's entry: Betsy Morris, "The Accidental CEO," *Fortune Online*, 9 June 2003, http://www.fortune.com/fortune

/print/o,115935,457272,00.html; Olga Kharif, "Anne Mulcahy Has Xerox by the Horns," *Business Week Online,* 29 May 2003, http://www.businessweek.com/technology/content/may23/tc20030529_1642_tc111.htm; Barbara Rose, "Firms Forced to Raise Offers to Retain Top Talent," *Greenwich Time*, 8 January 2006.

Day 3: The Shot Heard Around the World

1. The following sources were used in writing this day's entry: Phil Jackson and Hugh Delehanty, *Sacred Hoops: Spiritual Lessons of a Hardwood Warrior* (New York: Hyperion, 1995), 15–22; Phil Jackson, *The Last Season: A Team in Search of Its Soul* (New York: Penguin Press, 2004), 242–59.

Day 4: Soldier of Peace

1. The following sources were used in writing this day's entry: Howard Gardner and Emma Laskin, *Leading Minds: An Anatomy of Leadership* (New York: HarperCollins, 1995), 148–63; Carl Joachim Hambro, Nobel Peace Prize Presentation Speech—George C. Marshall, http://nobelprize.org/nobel_prizes/peace/laureates/1953/press.html; Charles Colson with Harold Fickett, *The Good Life: Seeking Purpose, Meaning, and Truth in Your Life* (Wheaton, IL: Tyndale House, 2005), 5; Geoffrey C. Ward, *American Originals: The Private Worlds of Some Singular Men & Women* (New York: Random House, 1994), 184–90.

Day 5: Hug Your Customers™

1. Based on a series of conversations between the author and Jack Mitchell and from Jack Mitchell, *Hug Your Customers: The Proven Way to Personalize Sales and Achieve Astounding Results.*

Week 2

Day 6: A Most Unlikely Turnaround

1. Schama, *A History of Britain: At the Edge of the World, 3500 B.C.–1603 A.D.* (New York: Miramax Books) 331–90.

Day 7: Enlightened Monarch?

1. The following sources were used in writing this day's entry: Burns, *Leadership*, 10, 27–28; Gaines, *Evening in the Palace of Reason,* 194–212, 245–48.

Day 8: First in Their Hearts

1. The following sources were used in writing this day's entry: Philip Kunhardt Jr., Philip Kunhardt III, and Peter W. Kunhardt, "The Heroic Posture," in *The American President,* videocassette (Alexandria, VA: PBS Home Video: Warner Home Video, 2000); *George Washington's Rules of Civility & Decent Behavour In Company and Conversation,* (Bedford, Maine: Applewood Books, 1988); Edward Lengel, e-mail message to the author, 8 April 2005; Bill Moyers, *A World of Ideas,* ed. Betty Sue Flowers (New York: Doubleday, 1989), 8–9, 229; Joseph J. Ellis, *His Excellency: George Washington* (New York: Alfred A. Knopf, 2004), xiv.

NOTES

Day 9: Reconnecting a Nation

1. The following sources were used in writing this day's entry: William J. Bennett, *The Moral Compass: A Companion to The Book of Virtues* (New York: Simon & Schuster, 1995) 687-690; Jay Winik, *April 1865: The Month That Saved America* (New York: HarperCollins, 2002), 183–91, 362–63; Ward, *American Originals: The Private Worlds of Some Singular Men & Women.*

Day 10: Connection to the Cause

1. David McCullough, *Brave Companions: Portraits in History* (New York: Prentice Hall, 1992), 37–51.

Week 3

Day 11: Community Catalyst

1. Howard Schultz and Dori Jones Yang, *Pour Your Heart into It: How Starbucks Built a Company One Cup at a Time* (New York: Hyperion, 1997).

Day 12: The Business of The Body Shop

1. The following sources were used in writing this day's entry: Bo Burlingham, "This Woman Has Changed Business Forever," *Inc.com,* June1990, http://inc.com/magazine/19900601/5201.html; Beth Carney, "Toning Up The Body Shop," *Business Week Online,* 18 May 2005, http://www.businessweek.com/bwdaily/dnflash/may2005/nf20050518_6631_db016.htm?chan=search.

Day 13: More Than an Oracle

1. The following sources were used in writing this day's entry: Monica Langley, "In Tough Times for CEOs, They Head to Warren Buffet's Table," *Wall Street Journal,* 1 November 14, 2003; Susan Pulliam and Karen Richardson, "Warren Buffett Unplugged," *Wall Street Journal,* weekend edition, 12–13 November 2005; Anthony Bianco, "The Warren Buffett You Don't Know," *Business Week Online,* 15 July 1999, http://www.businessweek.com/1999/99_27/b3636001.htm?script Framed; Carol Loomis, "The Value Machine," *Fortune,* 20 February 2001, www.fortune.com/fortune/subs/print/0,15935,373944,00.html; Andy Serwer, "The Oracle of Everything," *Fortune Online,* 27 October 2002, http://fortune.com/subs/print/0,15935,389954,00.html; also see the Berkshire Hathaway's Owner's Manual, http://www.berkshirehathaway.com.

Day 14: Ritz-Carlton Character and Culture

1. The following sources were used in writing this day's entry: Author's conversations with and e-mails from Ritz-Carlton employees; http://www.ritzcarlton.com; Matt Damsker, "Putting on the Ritz," *HR Innovator,* March 2004, 37–43.

Day 15: Peter Drucker's Kind of Leader

1. The following sources were used in writing this day's entry: John A. Byrne, "Profiting from the Nonprofits," *Business Week,* 26 March 1990, 66–74; Sally Helgesen, *The Female Advantage: Women's Ways of Leadership* (New York:

Doubleday, 1995), 71–103; Ani Hadjian, "Follow the Leader," *Fortune,* 27 November 1995, 96; Frances Hesselbein, "The Power of Civility," *Leader to Leader* 5 (Summer 1997), http:www.leadertoleader.org/leaderbooks/121/summer97/fh.htl.

Week 4

Day 16: Dr. Fred's INN

1. Fred Epstein, M.D., and Joshua Horwitz, *If I Get to Five: What Children Can Teach Us About Courage and Character* (New York: Henry Holt, 2003).

Day 17: Purpose-Driven Pastor

1. Gladwell, "The Cellular Church," 60–67.

Day 18: Patriot Playbook

1. The following sources were used in writing this day's entry: Judy Battista, "Patriots Adhere to Bottom Line to Stay on Top," *New York Times,* 8 August 2004; Charles Stein, "Bill Belichick CEO," *Boston Globe,* 28 January 2004; Alex Timiraos, "Pat's Coach Talks Leadership at BC," *The Heights,* 9 April 2004; Terry McDonell, "Quality of Effort," *Sports Illustrated,* 12 December 2005, 11; Charles P. Pierce, "The Ultimate Teammate," *Sports Illustrated,* 12 December 2005, 76–84.

Day 19: High-Five Moments

1. The following sources were used in writing this day's entry: Julie Bick, "Inside the Smartest Little Company in America," *Inc.,* January 2002, http://inc.com/magazine/20020101/23798.html; Clive Thompson, "The Play's the Thing," *New York Times Magazine,* 28 November 2004; "The Cranium Story: From Personal Mission to Global Movement," http://www.cranium.com; Paula Bock, "Playing for Fun and Profit," *Seattle Times,* 26 May 2006; Stephanie Dunnewind, "Seattle's Cranium Is Winning Awards with Innovative, Entertaining Play for All Ages," *Seattle Times,* 28 February 2004; Bruce Horovitz, "Cranium Guys Have Their Inner Child on Speed Dial," *USA Today,* 8 May 2006.

Day 20: Transforming the Culture of Kim

1. The following sources were used in writing this day's entry: Cynthia Coulson, "Kim Jeffery's Nestlé Waters Bottles Water Values," *Greenwich Magazine,* January 2003, 72–86; also see information at http://www.nestle-watersna.com.

Conclusion: Build a Fire That Lasts

1. McCullough, *Brave Companions: Portraits in History* (New York: Simon & Schuster), xiv.
2. John Wooden with Steve Jamison, *Wooden: A Lifetime of Observations and Reflections On and Off the Court* (New York: McGraw-Hill, 1997), 197.
3. Walton, "John Wooden, Like UCLA, Simply the Best."
4. Focus on the Family, 2004, "Coach Wooden: Timeless Wisdom," CD-ROM.
5. Arie de Geus, "The Living Company," *Harvard Business Review* (March–April 1997): 51–59.
6. Bill Thrall, Bruce McNichol, and Ken McElrath, *The Ascent of a Leader: How*

Extraordinary Relationships Develop Extraordinary Character and Influence (San Francisco: Jossey-Bass, 1999), 17.

7. Dr. J. Robert Clinton, "Listen Up Leaders! Forewarned Is Forearmed!" unpublished study, 1992. E-mail Dr. Clinton at JRClinton@aol.com to request a copy.
8. Diane L. Coutu, "Putting Leaders on the Couch: A Conversation with Manfred F. R. Kets de Vries," *Harvard Business Review* (January 2004): 65–71.
9. WorldofQuotes.com, http://www.worldofquotes.com/author/EdmundBurke/1.

ACKNOWLEDGMENTS

First, I want to acknowledge the contributions of my coauthors Carolyn Dewing-Hommes and Jason Pankau. Over the course of several years of ongoing research and writing, the three of us met most weeks to discuss our work. Their contributions were invaluable. So much so, in fact, that after a certain point I asked them to be coauthors. Other invaluable contributions came from Katie Stallard. Her thoughts about how to better communicate our ideas are reflected throughout this book.

While I was researching and writing this book, my wife, Katie, was treated for two different types of cancer. Throughout those periods, our family, friends, and health-care professionals provided tremendous support and encouragement. As I write in the Introduction, their connecting with us helped us make it through a challenging season. No words can express our gratitude for their love and support.

Many thanks also go to Don Pape and Alive Communications who brought our book proposal to Nelson Business. I am grateful to Brian Hampton at Nelson Business for believing in our book and assigning it to a talented editor, Bryan Norman. Bryan has become a trusted advisor and friend. His insights, suggestions, enthusiasm, and encouragement helped me persevere through the hard work and long hours to make a book on a complex subject more understandable and accessible to readers. Paula Major and Dimples Kellogg also made significant improvements to the book throughout the copyediting stage, and I thank them for their contributions.

A book of this sort is to some degree a community project. Carolyn, Jason, and I owe our thanks to those who shared their experiences and insights with us or otherwise encouraged and supported us on our journey to write this book. They include Susan Baisley, Mike Barriere, Hillary Bercovici, Rick Bibb, James Bliss, Bob Boiarsky, Camille Broderick, Barbara Casey, Deanna Castellini, Dorothea Cernera, Steve Cohen, Chris Combe, Eric Cooper, Ian Cron, Robbie de Villiers, Mitchell Dickey, Rich Ditizio, Matthew Ericksen, Mike Flatley, John Frelinghuysen, Gregory Furman, Tom Gavin, John Gration, Jerry Gerber, Beth Goldstein, Dr. Edward Hallowell, Lucy Hedrick, Frances Hesselbein, Carl Higbie, Vicki Ho, Linda Houston, Elmer and Esther Huh, Mark Hutchinson, Richard and Sandy Humphrey, Michelle Ian, J. Pendleton James, Cliff Johnson, Rasheed Kahn, Richard and Leslie Kaskel, Jennifer Kish, Steve Kerr, Walter Klores, Michael Kostoff, Ed Lengel, Chip Low, Mark Linsz, Rick Lyons, Tim Mackenzie, Regina Fazio Maruca, Rob Mathes and family, Dennis McDonnell, Sarah Meehan, Bruce McNichol, Jack Mitchell, William Molinari, Andrea Mueller, Richard and Wendy Murphy, David Myers, Michelle Newton, Joey Pierce, Joe Pine, Russell Reynolds, Jr., Wes Roberts, Kurt Reisenberg, Alex Rohman, Adam Rosenberg, Ken Runkel, Cecylia Rutkowska, Larry Sands, Matthew Sawyer, Marco Selva, Paul D. Speer Jr., Joseph Stallard, John Straus, Mark Taylor, Richard Tanaka and family, Khiem Ting, Elizabeth Toohey, Neely Towe, Dan Waters, Tom Wells, Stephanie Whittier, Sean Witty, Keith Vanderveen, and the staff of Greenwich Library.

I personally would like to thank my wife, Katie, and our daughters, Sarah and Elizabeth. I would also like to thank Clayton Dahlman, Holly Dahlman, MD, Bunny and John Harrison, Russ and Dorothy Hufstedler, Henry and Barbara Price, Robert Stallard, and Timothy Stallard.

Carolyn would like to thank her husband, Mark, for his never-ending support and his honest feedback over the years.

Also, she would like to thank her three children, Jessica, Daniel, and Catherine, for their patience and opinions all along the way.

Jason personally would like to thank his wife, Jennifer, and their children, Jarod, Jaden, Julianne, and Josephine. He would also like to thank Stanwich Congregational Church.

ABOUT THE AUTHORS

Michael Lee Stallard is the founder of E Pluribus Partners. Previously, he was managing director and chief marketing officer for the US Trust Company, and principal, chief marketing officer at the global private wealth management business of Morgan Stanley. The team he assembled and led at Morgan Stanley contributed to doubling the business unit's revenues over a two-year period. Earlier in his career, Michael gained broad business experience in marketing, finance, and business development-related positions at Texas Instruments, Van Kampen Merritt, and Barclays Bank, PLC.

Recognized as a thought leader in marketing and engaging people on the front lines of a business, Michael has spoken at various organizations, including conferences organized by *Fortune* magazine, the World Presidents' Organization, the American Bankers Association, the Corporate Executive Board's VIP Forum, and the Investment Company Institute. Along with his colleagues Carolyn Dewing-Hommes and Jason Pankau, he was a contributor to *What Managers Say, What Employees Hear: Connecting with Your Front Line (So They'll Connect with Customers)*, edited by Regina Maruca, a former senior editor of *Harvard Business Review.*

Michael received a BS degree in marketing from Illinois State University, an MBA from the University of Texas (Permian Basin), and a JD from DePaul University Law School. He was admitted to the Illinois bar in 1991.

Carolyn Dewing-Hommes, cofounder and partner at E Pluribus Partners, spent fifteen years at Citibank working in New York City, Sao Paulo, London, and Hong Kong. She was selected to lead a global team, reporting to Citibank's CEO, which identified the best practices of companies worldwide that successfully engaged their employees, specifically in the area of work/life balance. She received a BA in political science and languages from Georgetown University and a master's degree in economics and international affairs from Columbia University.

Jason Pankau, a cofounder and partner at E Pluribus Partners, is president of Lifespring Network, served as an associate pastor at Stanwich Congregational Church in Greenwich, Connecticut, where he focused on mentoring and leadership development. He was involved in starting two churches in Providence and Boston. He serves as a consultant and life coach to many corporate executives and pastors. He is sought as a speaker by organizations for his wisdom in teaching leadership and mentoring leaders. Jason earned a BS from Brown University in business economics and organizational behavior/management. Jason earned a Master of Divinity from Southern Theological Seminary. He is presently completing a doctorate degree in Christian leadership at Gordon-Conwell Theological Seminary.

E PLURIBUS PARTNERS

E Pluribus Partners is a Greenwich, Connecticut-based think tank focused on helping bring about greater connection among management, employees, and customers. The organization's name was derived from the motto of America, *E Pluribus Unum*, created by John Adams, Benjamin Franklin, and Thomas Jefferson. It means in Latin, "out of many, one." More information about E Pluribus Partners can be found at www.epluribuspartners.com.

INDEX

INDEX

INDEX

Printed in the United States
141927LV00001B/31/P